Toward a True
Kinship of Faiths

HIS HOLINESS

THE
DALAI
LAMA

TOWARD A TRUE
KINSHIP OF FAITHS

HOW THE WORLD'S RELIGIONS
CAN COME TOGETHER

Doubleday Religion

New York London Toronto Sydney Auckland

ꀃꀃ

DOUBLEDAY

Copyright © 2010 by His Holiness the Dalai Lama

Published in the United States by Doubleday Religion, an
imprint of the Crown Publishing Group, a division of Random
House, Inc., New York.
www.crownpublishing.com

DOUBLEDAY and the DD colophon are registered trademarks of
Random House, Inc.

"The Dark Night" from *The Collected Works of St. John of the Cross*,
translated by Kieran Kavanaugh and Otilio Rodriguez, copyright
©1964, 1979, 1991 by Washington Province of Discalced
Carmelites, is reprinted by kind permission of ICS Publications,
2131 Lincoln Road, N.E., Washington, DC, 20002-1199, U.S.A.,
www.icspublications.org.

"Mirabai Has Finished with Waiting" from *Mirabai: Ecstatic
Poems,* translated by Robert Bly and Jane Hirshfield, is reprinted
by kind permission of Beacon Press, Boston.

Library of Congress Cataloging-in-Publication Data
Bstan-'dzin-rgya-mtsho, Dalai Lama XIV, 1935–
    Toward a true kinship of faiths : how the world's religions can
come together / by the Dalai Lama. — 1st ed.
        p.   cm.
    Includes bibliographical references and index.
    (alk. paper)
    1. Religions.   2. Religions—Relations.   I. Title.
    BL85.B85 2010
    201'.5—dc22

                                    2009036771

ISBN 978-0-385-52505-3

Printed in the United States of America

10   9   8   7   6   5   4   3   2   1

First Edition

CONTENTS

PREFACE

Fifty years ago, a young man of twenty-four, I walked out of the Norbu Lingka palace in Lhasa, the capital of Tibet, with a gun slung over my shoulder. I was disguised as a bodyguard, wearing a *chuba*, the traditional Tibetan layman's costume, and without my glasses. With a small group I fled the city and began the journey to freedom and exile in India. The political circumstances that drove me into exile remain such that I have not been able to return.

Since that night of March 17, 1959, our world has changed almost beyond recognition—and certainly beyond the imagination of a Tibetan monk who had never been outside of Asia. Some of today's household words—*Internet, e-mail, digital camera, genome, AIDS, globalization, iPod*—had not even been coined. Today, the world we live in is truly global. No country can remain untouched by technological innovation, environmental degradation, the globalized systems of modern economics and banking, instant communications, and the World Wide Web. Furthermore, the pace of exchange in ideas and people—both tourists and refugees—has created unprecedented contact and closeness among the world's many cultures. Swiftly, the effects of what happens in one part of the world are felt everywhere else. Nowhere is immune. The challenge before us—much more urgent than in the past—in this era of nuclear weapons, international terrorism, financial uncertainty, and ecological crisis, is simply peaceful coexistence.

This challenge of peaceful coexistence, I believe, will define the task of humanity in the twenty-first century. As early as 1930, one of India's greatest modern visionaries saw the problems clearly. In his Hibbert Lectures at Oxford, Rabindranath Tagore wrote:

> The races of mankind will never again be able to go back to their citadels of high-walled exclusiveness. They are today exposed to one another, physically and intellectually. The shells, which have so long given them full security within their individual enclosures, have been broken, and by no artificial process can they be mended again. So we have to accept this fact, even though we have not yet fully adapted our minds to this changed environment of publicity, even though through it we may have to run all the risks entailed by the wider expansion of life's freedom.
>
> (THE RELIGION OF MAN, PP.141–42)

These sentiments are exactly to the mark. But the pressures on us now are far greater than when Tagore wrote.

In the face of the stresses caused by the confrontation with other cultures and ideas, and the rapidity of their effects on one's own world of such global events as the economic downturn, which in part originated elsewhere, it is not surprising that some have spoken of a "clash of civilizations." Personally, I find such talk disturbing and unhelpful, for it only serves to accentuate the potential for discord. There is another possibility. The pressure cooker of globalization can move humanity in another direction, to the deeper plane where peoples, cultures, and individuals can connect with their basic, shared human nature. In that place, it is possible for us human beings to recognize the global nature of the problems facing us and our shared responsibility to confront them together, and to affirm the oneness of our human family. If we do not, the very survival of our species is at stake.

One area where peaceful coexistence has been hugely problematic in the history of humankind is in the relations between the world's religions. In the past, conflicts generated by religious differences may have been significant and regrettable, but they did not threaten the future of the planet or the survival of humanity. In today's globalized world, where extremists have access to vast technological resources and can draw on the immense emotive power of religion, a single spark could ignite a powder keg of truly frightening proportions. The challenge before religious believers is to genuinely accept the full worth of faith traditions other than their own. This is to embrace the spirit of religious pluralism.

The line between exclusivism—which takes one's own religion to be the only legitimate faith—and fundamentalism is a dangerously narrow one; the line between fundamentalism and extremism is even narrower. The time has come for every individual adherent of a major world religion to ask: "What, in my heart of hearts, is my attitude to the followers of other faiths?" We, the believers, no longer have the luxury of the kind of tolerance that does not accord full respect to other religions. After 9/11, the upholding of exclusivist religious bigotry in today's world is no longer a private matter of an individual's personal outlook. It has the potential to affect the lives of all.

The lesson I draw is that understanding and harmony between the world's religions is one of the essential preconditions for genuine world peace.

Over the years I have come to recognize that I have three principal commitments in my life—one might even call them missions. First, as a human being, I am committed to the promotion of what I call basic human values, by which I mean especially compassion, which I see as the foundation of human happiness. Nurturing this compassionate seed within us and acting from this innate capacity are the keys to fulfilling the basic aspiration to happiness. There is an intimate connection between love and compassion, on the one hand, and genuine happiness, on the other. The indispensability of compassion touches us all, whether we are rich or poor, educated or uneducated, religious or nonreligious, from this nation or from that one. It is innate in us, the birthright of everyone born human. From our very first day in this life, we are wholly dependent on the love of our mother or some other caregiver. If we as a species are serious about creating a more caring and happier world, then it is this precious quality we need to foster and practice.

My second commitment, as a religious person, is to the promotion of inter-religious understanding and harmony. This book, which I have been so happy to write, is primarily aimed at contributing to this objective. Finally, my third commitment, as a Tibetan and as the Dalai Lama, is to the pursuit of a happy and satisfactory solution to the sad crisis of Tibet and its people. While the third commitment is an inherited one, bequeathed to me in my role as the Dalai Lama, the first two are voluntary—willingly and happily taken up by me—and will last until my final breath.

Despite the tremendous progress in material conditions the world over, suffering remains. The afflictions such as greed, anger, hatred, and envy that underpinned much of our misery thousands of years ago continue to do so even today. Unless there is a radical change in human nature within a rapid period of time, these afflictions will plague us for many centuries to come. The teachings of each of the world's great religions, in their own unique way, have been and will continue to be a spiritual resource to counter the effects of these afflictions. Therefore, religion remains relevant and will have an important role in human society for the foreseeable future. Supremely, the religions have inspired the flow of compassion and great acts of altruism, the effects of which have resonated in the lives of millions. So, both from the point of view of peace in the world and to foster the beneficial potential of religion in the world, the faith traditions must find a way of relating to each other with mutual acceptance and genuine respect.

This book attempts to outline the arena within which it may be possible to create the dialogue that can lead to genuine inter-religious understanding. As I look at the world today, I see dangerous forces of polarization. There are worrying trends within the religions to denigrate other faiths; there is also increasing polarization between the religious and those with no religion. Such attitudes will only harden mutual suspicion and distrust. Yet, I believe that those arguing for exclusivism are fundamentally misguided as to the essential ground on which a religious spirituality is based. It is the task of all human beings with an aspiration to spiritual perfection—not just the leaders of the world religions but also every individual believer—to affirm the fundamental value of the compassion that lies both at the heart of human nature and at the core of the ethical teachings of all the world's major religions. In this way we can truly develop a deep recognition of the value of other faiths, and on that basis, we can cultivate genuine respect.

When I came to India as a refugee in 1959, I knew very little about religions other than my own. In the last fifty years, I have spent a substantial part of my time and attention learning and thinking about the great world religions beyond my own Buddhism. This has been hugely uplifting, for it has affirmed for me the extraordinary richness of the human spirit when it comes to envisioning the ideal of perfection and examining the fundamental questions of existence. On the metaphysical level, all major religions confront the same perennial questions: Who am I? Where do I come from? Where will I go after death? On the level of living a good life, all the faith traditions turn to compassion as a guiding principle. They use different words, invoke different images, root themselves in different concepts. But what they have in common is far more than what divides them, and their differences form the potential for a tremendously enriching dialogue, rooted in a marvelous diversity of experience and insight.

This book attempts to explore these convergences while setting up a model where differences between the religions can be genuinely appreciated without serving as a source of conflict. The establishment of genuine inter-religious harmony, based on understanding, is *not* dependent upon accepting that all religions are fundamentally the same or that they lead to the same place. I do maintain, however, that their very different metaphysical teachings give, in each case, a truly inspiring foundation for a beautiful ethical system rooted in compassion. I have no doubt that a sincere believer can, with integrity, be a pluralist in relation to religions other than his own, without compromising commitment to the essence of the doctrinal teachings of his own faith.

My engagement with the world's religions has convinced me that, whatever the differences of doctrine, on the level of actually living a religious life or fulfilling a spiritual aspiration, there is a striking degree of shared understanding. In particular, all the great religions stress compassion as a fundamental spiritual value. Whether it is in scriptural prescriptions for leading a good life, in the ideal of life that is admired and propagated, or in the exemplary lives of many of the remarkable individuals of different faiths, past and present (some of whom I have been privileged to meet), I have no doubt that compassion lies at the heart of all these religions. If this is true, there is a tremendous potential for the world's religions to come together in the cause of human goodness. Yet the task is massively difficult. The history of religion seems fraught with discord, mutual suspicion, and ideological conflict rooted in bigotry and exclusivism, or the view that one's own faith is the only legitimate one. I believe that the underlying causes of this history of divisiveness have no defensible basis. The challenge before us—which I see as most urgent—is to overcome this history and move to a harmonious understanding rooted in compassion.

Although this book deals with the world's great religions, the story it tells is of one man's experience and of a personal engagement. I have no illusion that what is offered here does justice to the totality of any one religion, nor even succeeds in capturing its essential teachings as understood within the tradition itself. However, I sincerely hope that the story told here—of a Buddhist monk's journey into the world's religions—offers encouragement, perhaps even inspiration, to others to enter deeply into traditions different from their own.

I should like to thank the innumerable people from all the religions who have granted me their time and helped me to come to a deeper appreciation of the world's great teachings. From my personal conversations with India's religious masters, such as the Jain teacher Acharya Tulsi, to deep exchanges with Christian practitioners like the Trappist monk Thomas Merton, I have been accorded a tremendous privilege and a rare opportunity to enter the wonderful world of other faith traditions. In order that the reader is not taxed with too many names I shall not be able to list the names of so may of the religious leaders and practitioners I have been privileged to meet over so many years. To all of them, however, I owe deep personal gratitude for their time, wisdom, and compassion.

I have a boundless respect for my own Buddhist faith, but to see it within the context of its brother and sister religions has afforded me a vision of the grandeur and extent of what I truly believe to be the finest aspirations of the human spirit. My gratitude is also due to my two editors—Dr. Thupten Jinpa, who has been my principal translator now for a quarter of a century, and his colleague, Dr. Jaś Elsner—for helping me express my thoughts as cogently as possible in English, and especially for their help in selecting and checking citations from the world's scriptures. In the process of writing, the editors, as well as members of my own personal staff, have helped me think through the implications and consequences of some of the more challenging aspects of my ideas. I would also like to thank those individuals who have read and commented on the manuscript.

May the effort of this book be of benefit to the emergence of a genuine understanding between the world's great religions, and may it foster in us deep reverence toward one another.

Toward a True
Kinship of Faiths

LEAVING

THE COMFORT

ZONE

1956, The First Opening

When I was growing up in Tibet, and especially after my serious engagement in studies of classical Buddhist thought and practice from the age of fifteen, I used to feel that my own Buddhist religion was the best. I thought that there simply could not be any other faith tradition that could rival the depth, sophistication, and inspirational power of Buddhism. Other religions must, at best, be "so-so." Looking back, I feel embarrassed by my naïveté, although it was the view of an adolescent boy immersed in his own inherited religious tradition. Yes, I was vaguely aware of the existence of a great world religion called Christianity that propounds the way of salvation through the life of its savior, Jesus Christ. In fact, as a child I had heard the story of how some Christian priests had once established a mission in western Tibet in the seventeenth century. There was also a small community of Tibetan Muslims right up until modern times, who had lived in Lhasa city for over four centuries. As for Hindus and Jains, followers of the two other major religions native to India, I was convinced that the philosophical arguments, found in the classical Buddhist critiques of their tenets, had effectively demonstrated the superiority of the Buddhist faith centuries ago.

Needless to say such naïveté could be sustained only so long as I remained isolated from any real contact with the world's other religions. The first time I had any direct contact with a real Hindu was when a *sadhu*, an Indian holy man, with matted hair and white lines of ash painted on his forehead, appeared at the Potala Palace when I was a child. He was shouting "Dalai Lama, Dalai Lama!," and appeared to have wanted to see me. Of course, he spoke no Tibetan and nobody in the vicinity spoke any Hindi. There was quite a commotion as my attendants, bodyguards, and all sorts of onlookers tried to stop him! Nobody had any idea who or what he was, or from what religious background he came. The pivotal moment of contact came when I had the opportunity to visit India for the first time in 1956. Before this, the only other country I had been to was China, which was then in the full swing of communism.

It was the crown prince of Sikkim, in his capacity as the president of the Maha Bodhi Society, as well as the special committee set up by the government of India to organize the 2,500th anniversary of the Buddha's death, known as the *parinirvana*, who officially invited me to India. My spiritual colleague, the late Panchen Lama (who later suffered a lot in the wake of the communist takeover of Tibet yet did so much for the Tibetan people until his untimely death in Tibet in 1986), also joined me on this historic visit to India. During more than three months' stay in India at that time, I had the honor to meet many people from all walks of life, as well as from all kinds of religious backgrounds. The president of India, Dr. Rajendra Prasad, graciously engaged me in deep conversation on several occasions. A noted legal scholar, India's first president was also a deeply religious man who took seriously the historical legacy of India as a birthplace of some of the world's great religions. His humility and his deep humanity made me feel that in being with him I was in the presence of a truly spiritual man, a being dedicated to the ideal of a genuinely selfless life of service. India's vice president then was Dr. Sarvepalli Radhakrishnan, a famed scholar of Indian philosophy and religion. Speaking with him was like being treated to an intellectual feast. On the personal level, getting to know the president and vice president, as well as Pandit Jawaharlal Nehru, India's first Prime Minister, made me feel somehow close to the great being Mahatma Gandhi, whom we Tibetans used to call at that time Gandhi Maharaja (literally, "Gandhi, the Great King!").

One meeting that left an enduring memory was a surprise visit from a senior Jain master who came to see me with an assistant monk. I remember clearly being surprised by the asceticism of these two Jain monks. It was, I later came to know, part of their everyday lifestyle always to sit on hard surfaces and not on soft cushions. Since we were in an official guesthouse, there was hardly any furniture without soft padding on the seats. So, finally, the monks sat on the coffee table. We had a lengthy conversation on the similarities between Buddhism and Jainism, which historians often refer to as twin religions. Here, for the first time in my experience, was a real Jain practitioner whose articulation of his own faith tradition had little resemblance to the characterization of Jain views in the scholastic texts and refutations I had studied in my youth!

After the official celebrations of the Buddha's *parinirvana*, I was able to go on pilgrimage to the ancient Buddhist holy sites, especially Bodh Gaya, where the Buddha attained enlightenment; Lumbini, where he was born; and Sarnath, near Varanasi, where he preached his first sermon on the Four Noble Truths. Face-to-face with the holy *stupa* at Bodh Gaya and standing in front of the Bodhi Tree, which is descended from the very tree under which the Buddha attained enlightenment more than 2,500 years ago, I was moved to tears. This holy place is revered by Buddhists the world over—in Tibet there was even a custom of sculpting miniature models of the *stupa* at Bodh Gaya as objects of veneration. In my first autobiography, written soon after my going into exile in India, I described my emotions when I first saw the Bodh Gaya *stupa:*

> From my very early youth I had thought and dreamed about this visit. Now I stood in the presence of the Holy Spirit who had attained Mahaparinirvana, the highest Nirvana, in this sacred place, and had found for all mankind the path to salvation. As I stood there, a feeling of religious fervor filled my heart, and left me bewildered with the knowledge and impact of the divine power which is in all of us.

While on pilgrimage to the Buddhist sites in central India, I had the chance to witness a truly historic event. At Rajgir—where the tradition believes that the Perfection of Wisdom scriptures, so dear to the practitioners of Mahayana Buddhism, were originally taught—a grand ceremony took place in a colorful tent. Prime Minister Nehru had come to formally accept a gift to the people of India that was brought in person by the then Chinese premier, Zhou En-lai. This was a holy Buddhist relic that, I was told, had been brought to China from India in the seventh century, possibly by the famed Chinese pilgrim Xuán Tsang, and was now being returned to its original home. I felt so deeply honored to be present at this ceremony, which was what we Tibetans call a *tashipa*, or auspicious occasion. Nehru was agitated at the time because the Tibetan officials who accompanied me to India were divided in their thinking. One group suggested that I remain behind in India until the political situation inside Tibet became more settled, while the other group urged me to go back to Tibet and negotiate with the communist authorities in Beijing.

It was also during this Indian tour that I saw the famous Elephanta Caves, a historically significant sacred site for the Hindu tradition located just off the coast of Mumbai (Bombay). Dated to around the ninth century CE, this temple complex of caves contains many beautiful rock carvings of important divinities from the Hindu pantheon. The central image is a twenty-foot-high three-headed Shiva, whose three faces, I learned, represent the divinity in his three distinct but interconnected forms: the right face, which has a sensuous appearance, represents Shiva as the creator of the world; the left, which has an expression of anger, represents Shiva as the destroyer; while the central face, which has a gentle expression, symbolizes Shiva as the preserver of the universe.

As a Tibetan Buddhist, a follower of a tradition that takes great pride in its continuous lineage from the ancient Indian monastery of Nalanda, with its unsurpassed religious and philosophical legacy, to actually visit the site of Nalanda was truly memorable and moving. It was from here that came most of the great masters whose works are closely studied to this day in the Tibetan monastic colleges—works many of which I had myself studied as a young monk. In fact, one of the founders of Buddhism in Tibet, Shantarakshita, was a noted philosopher from Nalanda in the ninth century and the initiator of an important Buddhist school, the Yogacara Madhyamaka. Shantarakshita's classic *Tattvasamgraha* (Compendium of Epistemology) is highly admired to this day as a philosophical masterpiece, both in India and in Tibet. It was wonderful, too, to have the opportunity to pay homage to Nagarjunakonda in southern India, a monastic site associated with the great second-century Buddhist master Nagarjuna, to whom the Tibetan tradition refers as the "Second Buddha." By the 1980s, the monastery's actual location was under water, as a result of the construction of a large electrical dam near the site. Personally, being able to walk on the very site where Nagarjuna once lived was truly meaningful. Nagarjuna remains to this day one of the deepest sources of spiritual inspiration and philosophical insight for me.

Looking back to this trip in 1956, I realize that my visit to the Theosophical Society in Chenai (then Madras) left a powerful impression. There I was first directly exposed to people, and to a movement, that attempted to bring together the wisdom of the world's spiritual traditions as well as science. I felt among the members a sense of tremendous openness to the world's great religions and a genuine embracing of pluralism. When I returned to Tibet in 1957, after more than three months in what was a most amazing country for a young Tibetan monk, I was a changed man. I could no longer live in the comfort of an exclusivist standpoint that takes Buddhism to be the only true religion. When tragic political circumstances in 1959 forced me into exile in India to live as a refugee, I was paradoxically afforded the freedom to deepen my personal journey of understanding and engagement with the world's faith traditions.

Ironically, as political circumstances compelled me to move out of the physical comfort zone of my homeland of Tibet, my exposure to the grandeur of India's great religions brought me to let go of the mental comfort zone, a space where my own Buddhism was the one true religion and other faith traditions were at best mere similitude. As so often happens when we are confronted with tragedy and suffering, we come closer to reality—and this leaves little room for pretence and wishful thinking. Such were the circumstances as I began to establish my second home in India and helped to lay the foundation for the new lives of so many of my fellow Tibetans who came to India, Nepal, and Bhutan as refugees. On the personal level, this new situation—being a refugee and a guest of India during one of the darkest periods in Tibet's long history—brought with it a degree of freedom that I could never have imagined in my previous life as the head of a country, struggling under an ever-increasing loss of freedom. This new life allowed me to be what I call a "simple Buddhist monk," now free to forgo the ceremonial trappings that were such a pervasive aspect of the life of the Dalai Lama. I never really liked the ceremonies anyway, so I was happy to see them disappear. Perhaps, the most precious thing that this life in exile has brought me is the ability to meet so many people, especially ordinary people, from all backgrounds.

A Knock on the Door from the West

One remarkable person who crossed my path during my first decade of exile was a Christian monk who left a lasting impression. To this day, I vividly remember my meeting with Father Thomas Merton. He came to see me at my residence, in Dharamsala in northern India, in November of 1968. As a Trappist monk, Merton wore a white robe with a hood and a broad leather belt around his waist. In addition, he wore a pair of tall brownish boots, which looked quite out of place in Dharamsala. In appearance, nothing could be more striking than the contrast between our robes. As a Tibetan Buddhist monk, I wear maroon robes with a patch of golden yellow on my sleeveless vest. Our monastic robe is made of two pieces. The lower part is a robe that has several folds to allow easier movement of the legs when walking; this is tied with a sash around the waist. The upper part is a sleeveless vest with a loose shawl-like maroon cloth around it covering the left arm but leaving the right arm exposed. So, except for our hairstyle—in my case a shaved head and in Merton's case a natural baldness—there was hardly any similarity when it came to our appearance.

Merton's visit came at a perfect time. The initial task had been completed of ensuring the rehabilitation of the thousands of Tibetans who had fled mainly to India in the wake of my escape. The other priority for my community—the establishment of Tibetan schools for our refugee children—had also been accomplished, thanks to the kindness of the Indian government. So, the period from the mid 1960s to the end of that decade happened for me personally to be a wonderful time of critical reflection, spiritual contemplation, and meditation practice. In particular, I was able to revisit the great texts that I had studied in Tibet and delve into a series of new teachings and practices. I also had the opportunity to dedicate weeks at a time—sometimes even a month or two—to deepening my meditation practice and to philosophical reflection. My two tutors were with me in Dharamsala, as were several other great Tibetan masters who provided wise counsel when needed. So I spent many hours in meditative cultivation of universal compassion, as well as in deepening my understanding and experience of emptiness—the truth of the profound interdependent nature of all things—that the Nalanda tradition understands to be the ultimate reality. When Thomas Merton came to see me, I was able to explore deeply with him, in a series of conversations, some personal spiritual experiences on my part.

Merton was a robust man, both in the physical sense—he had a bodily frame with big bones—and in the spiritual sense. In him I saw a monk who cared deeply for the world, passionately believed in the power of spirituality to heal the wounds of humanity, and had an intense spiritual search. An advocate of inter-religious dialogue, Thomas Merton would penetrate into the realms of other faith traditions—Buddhism, in the case of discussion with me—so that he could, as it were, taste the actual flavor of the teachings that other traditions represent. For me, there was a real inspiration in Merton's engagement with Buddhism in that it reflected great courage on his part to explore traditions beyond his own. In our discussions, every now and then he would cast a deep, penetrating gaze at me, suggesting the full awareness of his presence in our conversation.

There is no doubt that my meeting with Thomas Merton opened my eyes to the richness and depth of the Christian faith. Later I found out that there were quite striking similarities between our lives. At his monastery, Merton's day began at 2:30 AM, while mine begins at 3:30 AM. He, too, spent many hours in the morning in contemplative prayer and silence, and had his breakfast early, which I do as well. Merton was a great and deeply knowledgeable advocate of inter-religious dialogue while remaining true to his own Christian faith. He, too, was a proponent of harmony among the followers of the world's great religions, based on a deep understanding of each other's profound spiritual teachings. Of course, as a monk, like me, he led a life dedicated to celibacy and service to others.

The key thing I learned from Merton was his profound clarity on a point that I have thought about many times since and have come to share deeply. Merton told me, and this is something he later published in his *Asian Journal,* that we, as a community of practitioners in the world religions, "have reached a stage (long overdue) of religious maturity at which it may be possible for someone to remain perfectly faithful to a Christian and Western monastic commitment and yet to learn in depth from say a Buddhist discipline and experience." Exactly the same is true from the Buddhist side as well. And, indeed, I have come to think that the essence of genuine interreligious dialogue must be founded on this conviction.

With Thomas Merton's tragic accidental death in Thailand at the age of fifty-three, only weeks after I met him, the world lost a truly spiritual man who had so much to offer, especially in the critical area of inter-religious understanding and harmony, as well as understanding between the perspectives of the faithful and the wider secular world. On a personal level, I lost a friend, an important ally in the promotion of inter-religious dialogue, and a mentor.

Almost twenty years later, I finally had the opportunity to visit Merton's monastery, Gethsemani Abbey in Kentucky. It was deeply moving to see where he lived, especially his cell, which was quite bare and austere, reflecting the ideal of a true monk who is dedicated to silence, tranquillity, and awakening. The simplicity of his life brings to mind a Tibetan expression: "In relation to oneself, few needs and few tasks; in relations to others, many needs and many tasks." Since then, I have visited Gethsemani again during a series of Christian-Buddhist monastic dialogues with participants from different Christian monastic orders, as well as Tibetan Buddhist monks.

Some Echoes from Tibet's Past

Later, looking back into the history of Tibet, I realized that Tibetan Buddhism had encountered Christianity as early as the seventeenth century. The then Guge kingdom in western Tibet had allowed a Goa-based community to open a mission in Tsaparang, where the foundation stone for the first Christian church in Tibet was laid in 1626. One of the priests who came to Tibet as a missionary toward the beginning of the eighteenth century was an Italian by the name of Ippolito Desideri. Remarkably, Father Desideri was able to spend almost twelve years in central Tibet, most of it in the capital city of Lhasa. Fascinated by the complexity of Buddhist thought and religious practice, this Jesuit not only mastered the Tibetan language but also embarked on a rigorous study of some of the key Buddhist texts that form the heart of the academic curriculum in the scholastic monasteries. It is said that Desideri established friendships with many monks from the great monastic university of Sera, which lies on the outskirts of Lhasa city, and that he would engage in hours of debate and discussion with them.

It turns out that, during his stay in Lhasa, Desideri composed a lengthy text in Tibetan. His book uses the model of many Tibetan Buddhist scholastic works, which typically treat a key topic within the framework of three broad headings: 1. refutation of the standpoint of others; 2. positing of one's own standpoint; and 3. rebuttal of objections against one's own standpoint raised by others. The work presented his critique of the key Buddhist theories of karma, rebirth, and emptiness. Then, remarkably using Buddhist philosophical language and phraseology, he argued for the Christian doctrine of the Holy Trinity and dealt with possible objections against this doctrine that might be raised from the Buddhist philosophical standpoint. Desideri's original text, handwritten by him in Tibetan, survives to this day in the Vatican library, I am told. Although he came originally as a missionary, intent to convert the Tibetans to Christianity, Desideri's experience of immersion in Tibetan culture produced a remarkable and very early testament to inter-religious dialogue. According to a Tibetan scholar who has read Desideri's text (which is as yet unpublished), the work begins with a robust argument for the value of comparative religious study. For example, I am told that Desideri argues that if one finds a convergence of one's own tradition with another, this can serve as an indirect affirmation of both. He uses the image of a tree watered by different sources— rain water, a stream, and so on—where the tree resembles the human soul while the water represents the different spiritual traditions that can sustain and nurture it. I hope that one day a translation and a careful study of this important document will be undertaken to make it available to the wider world. In later years, on a trip to Italy, I made a point of visiting the monastery from which Desideri originally came.

In delving so deeply into the philosophy and practice of Buddhism, at a time when the notion of inter-religious dialogue, especially with a major Asian religion was, to say the least, alien, Desideri was truly a pioneer in the field. I see him as an early precursor of Thomas Merton.

Among my Tibetan predecessors, perhaps the monk who had the closest encounter with the Abrahamic religions was Palden Yeshe, the Sixth Panchen Lama, who was one of the most prominent spiritual leaders in Tibet in the eighteenth century. Palden Yeshe's mother was from Ladakh, in northern India, and because of this he spoke Hindi fluently. It is said that he enjoyed engaging on a regular basis in long conversations on religion and philosophy with

scholars and practitioners of different faiths. In fact, his establishment at Tashi Lhunpo Monastery supported a community of more
than a score of assorted religious teachers—Hindus, Muslims, and
Christians—and his immediate officials included a few Hindus and
Muslims. The Sixth Panchen Lama also established a longstanding
friendship with the British officer George Bogle, through whom he
was able to hear about the modern scientific and technological
world. Bogle is supposed to have brought to Tashi Lhunpo, at the
personal request of the Panchen Lama, an assortment of scientific
instruments, including a telescope. It is a pity that the Panchen
Lama's engagement with the scholars and practitioners of other
faith traditions remained a personal pursuit and did not have a
wider impact on the Tibetan Buddhist establishment. It would have
been wonderful if Palden Yeshe had chosen to write something
about his personal views on the convergence and divergence of
Buddhism and the world's other great traditions, especially the
Abrahamic faiths.

There is an intriguing legacy that came out of the Panchen
Lama's engagement with Islam, however. A short text attributed to a
Muslim named Palu Ju appeared in Tibetan and became hugely popular among the ordinary people in Tibet, as it remains to this day.
Written in verse in a strong vernacular style, this "counsel from an
old Muslim" begins with a salutation that includes the following
lines:

*In Tibetan language you're known as Konchok Rinpoche (the Precious
Jewel),*
In my language you're known as Qudha (Allah), to you I pay my homage.

This poem weaves the essence of ethical teachings that are common
to both Buddhism and Islam in simple language. It speaks of the

need to distinguish between one's well-being in this life and the more important life beyond. The text suggests that the essence of spiritual practice lies in establishing a basis of happiness for all; it shows how the consideration of others' welfare is an important ethical precept, and how serving others constitutes the heart of religion. Many have suspected that the author of this work was the Sixth Panchen Lama himself, or one of the scholar monks closely associated with his inner circle. In any case, it is so popular that even illiterate Tibetans know lines from it by heart. I remember how some of the sweepers at the Potala Palace, who were my playmates when I was a boy, used to recite lines from it. One of their favorites, which has virtually become a Tibetan proverb, goes:

> *I, Musalman Palu, have said what is my heart's counsel;*
> *Whether you listen or not depends on your mind.*

Clearly, when the Tibetan lama Phakpa was in the Mongol Yuan court as the principal priest of Kublai Khan in the thirteenth century, he must have crossed paths with religious figures of other traditions, including the Abrahamic ones. Nestorian Christians remained active in central Asia for many centuries, while Catholics like Marco Polo were present at Kublai's court. Many central Asian communities had by the end of the twelfth century adopted Islam as their dominant faith. Of course, when Kublai conquered China, the country had a rich range of indigenous religious traditions—not only Confucianism and Daoism but also Buddhism. So, Phakpa Lama must have had exposure to the teachings and practices of many of the world's religions within the Khan's domain. Unfortunately, again we have no record in Tibetan of Phakpa Lama's engagement with other religions, nor do we have any text that artic-

ulates Phakpa's views regarding other faith traditions. As more literature from this period in other languages comes to light, perhaps we
will gain some understanding of the intricacies of the interrelations
among the various religions in Yuan China.

In terms of literary accounts of the views of other religions, the
Tibetan tradition has a long history of studying so-called doxogra-
phies *(druptha)* — that is, discussions of the philosophical tenets of all
the major classical Indian schools both Buddhist and non-Buddhist.
As a young man, I remember reading the early twelfth century text
by Üpa Losel that presents in quite some detail the views of many
non-Buddhist Indian sects. The most extensive among these Tibetan
doxographical works is that of the seventeenth-century author Jam-
yang Shepa, widely known for *An Extensive Exposition of the Philosophical Systems,* which I had studied in my youth.

It is within this genre of literature that we find the remarkable
text *The Crystal Mirror of Philosophical Systems,* a comparative history
of Asian religions and philosophies, by the eighteenth-century Tibetan author Thuken Chökyi Nyima. In this book, Thuken dealt
with the origin and the key tenets of the traditions that are native to
the Asian continent. The book is divided into three parts. Part One
deals with the religions and philosophies of classical India. Beginning with the presentation of the Vedic traditions, such as the five
classical Brahmanical schools of ancient India as well as Jainism,
Thuken then proceeds with a clear account of the doctrines of the
four principal classical schools of Indian Buddhism. Part Two presents in some detail the origin and development of the main Tibetan
schools, including the pre-Buddhist Bön tradition. The final part includes a brief presentation of the history and an account of the religions of China, especially Daoism and Confucianism, as well as
Chinese Mahayana Buddhism. In writing about the development of

Confucianism in China, Thuken notes the fact that the adherents of Confucianism tend to relate to their tradition more as an ethical teaching than as a religion. He acknowledges that many of the important religious themes characteristic of Asian religions, such as bondage and salvation, life after death, and karma, do not feature in Confucianism, and that the central teachings of the key texts of Confucianism, such as Confucius' (fifth century BCE) The Analects and Mencius' (third century BCE) *Meng-tzu* (The Book of Mencius), are best understood as presenting a system of humanistic ethics. Given the far-reaching impact of the Confucian teachings—spiritual, cultural, and political—in China and in other East Asian societies, Thuken considered Confucius and Mencius to be great spiritual teachers.

For me, one of the most attractive aspects of Confucianism is its advocacy of the notion that basic human nature is good. Remarkably, Mencius goes even so far as to argue that because human nature is good, love is an inborn moral quality. Like Buddhists, Mencius understood that this quality of love can be cultivated and enhanced through practice. He insisted that the practice of love must start with one's family, echoing the Buddha's teaching on *maitri* (loving-kindness), where one cultivates loving-kindness by first focusing on a loved one and then gradually extending that feeling to an ever wider circle of beings, including even one's enemy.

The other major ancient Chinese tradition presented by Thuken is Daoism. The Chinese word *Dao* (or *Tao*) means "path" or "way," and Daoist ethical teachings emphasize what are called the "Three Jewels of the Dao": compassion, moderation, and humility. According to this tradition, this Dao, or the Way, is the One Truth, which is both the beginning of all things and the way in which all things pursue their course. In Daoism, there is a great emphasis on spontaneity and action in accord with nature. Thuken admits that he had not read the great texts of Daoism, but he mentions both of Daoism's two great teachers, Lao Tzi and Zhuangzi. He even refers to Zhuangzi's famous puzzle about whether he is a man dreaming that he is a butterfly or a butterfly dreaming that it is a man. Thuken speaks also of the deification of Lao Tzi and the Daoist tradition attributing some eighty-one incarnations to the teacher, somewhat in the manner of the incarnations of the Hindu god Vishnu. Thuken was a native of Amdo province, where I was myself born, close to mainland China, as well as being a principal student of the great master Cankya Rolpai Dorje—a personal friend of the Qing emperor Quan-long. Thuken's treatment of the religions of China was based on personal contacts with practitioners of the respective traditions. Needless to say, reading about these great Chinese traditions in Tibetan at a young age was a source of deep wonder for me.

Looking back I see that, my crucial learning experience was the shift that took place away from a parochial and exclusivist vision of my own faith as unquestionably the best. Such a view is understandable in one who has insufficient experience and exposure, and may even be laudable in demonstrating a deep respect for one's own tradition. But it has elements of self-congratulation and even a kind of arrogance born of ignorance. The move to a pluralist position of interchange with other religions by no means involves abandoning one's central commitment to one's own faith; it hugely enriches the understanding and practice of one's own religion, as Desideri argued. It allows one to see convergences with other religions, to sharpen one's grasp of one's own tradition by seeing its specific and distinctive characteristics by way of contrast, and to broaden one's respect for the extraordinary range and diversity of spiritual approaches developed by humankind entirely outside of one's faith tradition. This book tells the story of how my own journey into inter-religious understanding, which began in 1956, came to unfold over the course of more than half a century, taking me into the beginning of a new millennium.

2

LIVING

IN A PLURALITY

OF FAITHS

India, the Birthplace of Great Religions

India became my second home in 1959. I have lived most of my adult life in this great subcontinent, which we Tibetans have historically referred to as the "Land of the Noble Ones." India still inspires awe in me, especially when I reflect on its long cultural and religious history. It is one of the few places on earth where great cities that date back before the dawn of the Common Era—Pataliputra (Patna) and Varanasi (Benares), for example—still thrive as vibrant communities. It is a country where millions have chanted the sacred lines from the Vedas for thousands of years, where the great rivers such as the Ganges, Yamuna, and Kaveri are still revered. In every major metropolitan city in India, you can see people of all faiths commuting, working, studying, and eating together. In almost every district of an Indian city, there are Hindu temples colorfully adorned with divine figures, clean and austere Jain temples, mosques with towering minarets, and churches with bells. This is the land of such recent luminaries of the human spirit as Mahatma Gandhi, Rabindranath Tagore, and Vinoba Bhave. Every time I return from an overseas trip, I feel at home and, as it were, a sense of connectedness with an old and mature soul.

If I ask myself what essentially I am at home with, I think it is the extraordinary tolerance and welcoming nature of India. Not only has it seen the birth of four of the world's great religions—Hinduism, Buddhism, Jainism, and Sikhism—but it has provided a home for so many others. Islam especially achieved an extraordinary flowering in India in philosophy, religious practice, and artistic creativity— indeed, India contains, after Indonesia, the world's second-largest Muslim population. Zoroastrianism, originally the great religion of ancient Persia, found a second home in India, while both Judaism and Christianity have also flourished as well.

For Buddhists, within India's great historical heritage, nothing can rival the fact that it gave birth to our cherished Buddhadharma, the "Way of the Awakened One." It was in Kapilvastu that the Buddha was born more than 2,500 years ago. It was in Bodh Gaya, under the Bodhi Tree in the Magadha kingdom, that the Buddha became fully enlightened. It was in Sarnath, near Varanasi, that the Buddha gave his first public sermon, which is known as the "first turning of the wheel of Dharma." So many of the places that are closely associated with the Buddha's life—his establishment of a monastic community, his sojourn during numerous rainy-season retreats, and his final passing into nirvana—that have so much meaning for devout Buddhists, are found in central India. I remember vividly when in 1956 I first stood in front of the sacred *stupa* in Sarnath. Being there, in front of the *stupa* within the ruins of the monastery that is known to the ancient Buddhist scriptures as the "Deer Park," tears came to my eyes as it struck me that here, on this very site, the Awakened One delivered his first public teaching on the Four Noble Truths. Having gained profound personal insight into the fundamental nature of human existence, the Buddha made it possible for others to share in his enlightenment by teaching the path. He declared that suffering is our reality, that suffering has an origin in karma and the afflictions, that there is a possibility for the cessation of suffering, and that there exists a path that leads to this cessation.

Central to the Buddha's realization was to see clearly that everything we do or think creates the psychological reality we live in—our sense of happiness or sorrow—and this then brings into being the pattern of our actions and thoughts. In the words of the opening verses of the Dhammapada:

Fore-run by mind are mental states,
Ruled by mind, made of mind.
If you speak or act with corrupt mind,
Sorrow follows you, as the wheel the foot of the ox.

Fore-run by mind are mental states,
Ruled by mind, made of mind.
If you speak or act with clear mind,
Happiness follows you, like a shadow that does not depart.

(THE DHAMMAPADA I:1–2)

This means that we have it in our own hands to bring about our own happiness and to overcome our own suffering. Like the teachings of other great traditions, those of the Buddha are in one way or another directed to the achievement of this goal. According to the Buddha, the path to salvation lies in the individual's taming his or her mind and perfecting the qualities inherent in the heart. Hence, he states:

> You are your own master,
> Who else will be your master?
> The wise who has become his own master,
> He shall accomplish his aims.
>
> (UDANAVARGA 23:10)

The Buddha's insight—that much of our suffering comes from our own untamed states of mind, dominated by afflictions such as greed, aversion, and delusion, and that the way to freedom lies within ourselves—has left a powerful imprint on India's spiritual landscape. Already, during his lifetime, many people had heeded the Buddha's message of self-reliance and the need to tame one's own mind and heart as the essence of a spiritual path. By the time the Buddha passed away at the age of eighty-one, his community, known as the Sangha, had already spread widely throughout central India. Less than two hundred years after his death, Ashoka, the great emperor who conquered large parts of India, embraced the Buddha's Dharma and proclaimed the essence of the Buddha's ethical teachings to the furthermost corners of his kingdom, which included modern-day Pakistan and Afghanistan. Some of the stone pillars on which Ashoka's edicts were carved can still be seen in remarkable condition in various museums. This includes a wonderful one in Sarnath, famous for its smooth marble surface topped with a capital composed of four lions. Over time, Buddhism spread across the entire Indian subcontinent, from Ghandhara (which lay in what is today Afghanistan and parts of Pakistan) in the north to the island-nation of Sri Lanka at the southernmost tip of India, from Kamarupa (modern-day Assam) in the east to the western regions that are now Rajasthan and Maharashtra. Briefly put, two great streams arose within Buddhism that can be described, on the basis of the primary languages in which their scriptures were transmitted, as the Pali tradition and the Sanskrit tradition. The former flourished in Sri Lanka, Burma, Thailand, and other countries in Southeast Asia, while the Sanskrit tradition spread north into central Asia and China along the Silk Road to Tibet and east to Korea, Japan, Indonesia, and Vietnam.

The embracing of Buddhism by the Greek Bactrians (the descendants of the soldiers of Alexander the Great) gave rise to the flowering of a vibrant tradition of Buddhist art with strong Greek Hellenistic influence, encapsulated in the Gandhara style of Buddhist images. In Lahore, Pakistan, not very far from my residence at Dharamsala, is a remarkable Gandhara statue of the Buddha as an ascetic, with the bones of his spine showing through his belly. I keep a photograph of this icon on my personal shrine to remind me of the intense, single-pointed effort that must underlie the path to full enlightenment. Even though the Buddha would come to reject extreme asceticism, for me this is the most inspiring icon of the Buddha because it powerfully reminds us of the hardships that cannot be avoided on a spiritual path.

With the establishment of major monasteries and centers of learning like Taxila (known also as Takshashila) in modern-day Pakistan and Nalanda, Ottantapuri, and Vikramalashila in central India, came an era of creative philosophical and intellectual inquiry into almost every aspect of human existence. From the study of logic and epistemology to the esoteric aspects of astronomy, from medicine to the subtle workings of the human mind, the scholars in these centers of learning debated, refined, and recorded their insights in works of great enduring quality. To this day, the thinking and writings of such masters as Nagarjuna (second century), Asanga (fourth century), Vasubandhu (fourth century), Dharmakirti (seventh century),

Candrakirti (seventh century), and Shantideva (late seventh to eighth century) retain their relevance for serious thinkers and practitioners of the Buddhist faith.

It is this rich philosophical heritage of Indian Buddhism, especially the tradition that thrived at Nalanda—the monastery described so well in Xuán Zàng's travel writings—that we Tibetans inherited when Buddhism came to flourish in our country in the seventh century. This Nalanda tradition makes up the core of my own philosophical, intellectual, and religious worldview. In fact, Tibet's cultural indebtedness to classical India goes well beyond the heritage of Buddhism. From Sanskrit poetics to the sciences, such as astronomy and medicine, from architecture to artistic forms, the influence of Indian civilization on classical Tibetan culture is significant. Even the Tibetan script is based on a form of old Indian writing that was current around the seventh century CE during the Gupta dynasty, when Buddhism came from India to Tibet. When I first saw some of the Gupta inscriptions in a museum in Patna, I was surprised that I could read many of the characters as if they were Tibetan!

Jainism: Buddhism's Twin Sibling

One important spiritual path to emerge in India around the same time as Buddhism is Jainism. The word *Jaina* literally means a "follower of the *Jinas* (Conquerors)." The teacher, a contemporary of the Buddha who formally founded Jainism, was Lord Mahavira. According to the Jains' own tradition, Mahavira is actually recognized as the last Jina in a line of twenty-four special beings, so their system traces its origin way back into the ancient past. In appearance, Lord Mahavira is represented like the Buddha—both teachers are depicted cross-legged in a meditative posture, both sport crown protrusions called *ushnisha* in Sanskrit, and both are seated upon a lotus. One iconographic difference is that Mahavira has a small mark on his heart that resembles a small lotus.

On the doctrinal and philosophical level, Jainism and Buddhism share many key ideas with other classical Indian schools. These include the concepts of karma, rebirth, *(samsaric)* unenlightened existence, and its transcendence in the form of freedom *(moksha)*. However, what marks Jainism and Buddhism as separate from other classical Indian traditions is their rejection of the priestly authority of the Brahmins, as well as the scriptural authority of the Vedas, a set of ancient scriptures deeply revered by the Hindus. On the philosophical level, like Buddhism, Jainism does not propound the notion of a Transcendent Being as the creator of all things. The universe has no beginning, nor an end. In other words, there is no concept of God in Jainism, and in this respect, like Buddhism, it is a nontheistic religion. Contrary to Buddhism, however, Jainism espouses the notion of self as an eternal principle that underlies the identity of the person as well as accounts for the continuity of a person across many lifetimes.

I particularly admire Jainism for its extraordinary emphasis on the need to respect all forms of life, and for enshrining the ethical conduct of nonkilling as strictly binding on its followers. Not only is a devout Jain a strict vegetarian, but often he or she would also avoid eating those vegetables that grow underground, such as onions, as their extraction inevitably involves the killing of many insects. The Jain monastic community is even stricter in its observance of this principle of nonkilling. Jain monks often wear a cloth around their mouths so that when they breathe out, the warm air does not accidentally kill organisms that are invisible to the naked eye!

Jainism has two main denominations, Digambara and Svetambara, and the followers of the first (which flourishes mostly in southern India) adopt a stricter ascetic lifestyle. The monks in this tradition remain naked—in fact, the word *digambara* literally means "sky-clad"—and avoid any activity that would involve creating karma and engendering further attachment. At an important religious event connected with Jainism, I once sat next to a Digambara ascetic who was completely naked. I was moved to see the total abandonment, courage, and depth of ascetic commitment in his lifestyle and I wondered what it would take for me to break through my own prejudices of custom to be able to go naked like him. In humility, I paid homage to him and touched my forehead to his knees. The followers of Svetambara wear coverings made of seamless white cloth. The dedication of some of these Jain monks in their pursuit of the purification of the soul inspires deep admiration; they are a model for any religious person who believes in the ideal of true spiritual freedom.

As I mentioned earlier, I first met a Jain practitioner in person on my visit to India in 1956. During this tour I was honored to meet one of the greatest twentieth-century Jain teachers, Acharya Tulsi, whom I had the privilege to know better during the years of my exile. Acharya was a truly great being, a Mahatma ("great soul") as one would say in Hindi. On Acharya's gracious invitation, I visited his monastery in Rajasthan to spend time at this deeply spiritual center. Through our conversations I came to see in this great being a kindred soul; he was a passionate advocate of nonviolence, an important value shared by all ancient Indian spiritual traditions and called *ahimsa* in Sanskrit, and he deeply believed that lasting world peace could come only through the promotion of nonviolence. Acharya also believed that, as great advances are made in human knowledge in the fields of science, it is extremely important that there be a close dialogue between science and spirituality so that both can serve humanity in the most positive manner. He once remarked at a world conference on peace and nonviolence in Rajasthan, India, which I also attended, "Both peace and war originate in the minds of men," and he emphasized the need to pay more attention to transforming the human psyche.

On the personal level, Acharya lived the life of a Jain ascetic. He shunned material comfort; as a Jain monk, he took seriously the vow of being a wanderer and undertook many barefoot walks across India. Yet in public life, Acharya was fully engaged with the world, especially through his commitment to social justice. I was particularly struck by his stress on the essence of Dharma practice as the purification of one's character and that the ritual aspects of the practice are secondary, a sentiment I have often expressed to my fellow Buddhists. I discovered that we also shared the view that the practice of religion is not meant only for bringing happiness in the afterworld, but is also a means of achieving genuine happiness in this very life.

Another giant in twentieth-century Jain history was Acharya Sushil Kumar, whom I met on numerous occasions. More than his contemporary, Acharya Tulsi, Sushil Kumar, who is affectionately referred to by his admirers as "Guruji" ("Honored Teacher"), was most active in the world. In fact, I later came to learn that he caused a stir within the Jain community when he embarked on an international tour in 1975. This is because Jain monks generally observe the practice of traveling strictly by foot. Guruji was a great advocate of inter-religious dialogue, and he presided over a session at the World Parliament of Religions conference in Chicago in 1993, where I was a participant. I remember that our final public meeting in the evening of the last day took place outside in a park, and over thirty-five thousand Chicagoans attended. This was wonderfully encouraging, as it suggested a high level of interest in inter-religious harmony even among the public. One of the most remarkable things that Guruji did was to speak out forcibly against the growing chorus of opposition to a visit by the late pope, John Paul II, to India. He reminded the people of India of that country's historical legacy as the birthplace of a plurality of religions and he appealed to them to welcome the pope with open arms.

Like Buddhism, Jainism does not explain the origin of the world in terms of a creator God. The law of causality, including the theory of karma (which literally means "action"), assumes fundamental significance for the worldview of both religions, since it provides the explanatory framework for understanding the origin of things. The mechanism by which karma works is understood differently in the two traditions, however. Roughly put, Jainism proposes that when a karmic act is committed—whether verbal, physical, or mental—this causes subtle particles of matter to stick to the person's soul. As these particles accumulate, they weigh the soul down and cause the individual to be continually reborn in a cycle of births. Buddhists, by contrast, explain this mechanism in a very different way—in fact, one finds a range of positions, not all of them compatible! For example, the great Nalanda masters maintain that once the specific karmic act is done, being an event, the act itself ceases immediately. However, the event leaves an imprint on the consciousness of the individual, which is carried until it comes to be ripened through activation by afflictive mental states, such as attachment and grasping at continued existence. Needless to say there has been much refinement of this view over the centuries.

Sikhism: Transcendence of Hindu-Muslim Dichotomy

A remarkable new religious movement—new by Indian standards—
that emerged on Indian soil is the Sikhism of the sixteenth century.
The first teacher in this tradition was Guru Nanak (1469–1539), who
was born in a village near Lahore in modern-day Pakistan. From his
youth, Guru Nanak was famed for his deeply compassionate character.
It is said that he would give away the merchandise his father had sent
him to sell to any beggar he happened to meet on the road. The era of
Guru Nanak in India witnessed a rise in the number of syncretistic religious movements, led by such figures as the Muslim weaver Kabir
(1398–1448) before his birth and the Hindu Brahmin Eknath
(1533–1599) after him. These teachers propounded the ultimate identity of Allah, Brahma, Vishnu, and other deities who may be characterized in distinct terms on the level of language. They discouraged
any emphasis on caste differences and argued that minor differences
in rituals have little significance—what matters is the awakening of
our innate pure nature. The point is beautifully caught in a poem by
Kabir, who was one of the greatest poets to write in Hindi:

O Servant, where does thou seek Me?
Lo! I am beside thee.
I am neither in temple nor in mosque: I am neither in Kaaba nor in
Kailash:
Neither am I in rites and ceremonies, nor in Yoga and renunciation.
If thou art a true seeker, thou shalt see Me: thou shalt meet Me in a
moment of time.
Kabir says, "O Sadhu! God is the breath of all breath."

(SONGS OF KABIR I.13 TRANSLATED BY RABINDRANATH TAGORE)

Though a follower of Kabir, Guru Nanak studied the sacred Vedas at the feet of many Hindu masters and went on pilgrimage to Mecca. One day, at the age of thirty-one, as he was bathing in a river, Guru Nanak mysteriously disappeared. Upon his reappearance three days later, he proclaimed that God is neither Hindu nor Muslim, and that he himself would follow God's way. Combining the essence of the two great religions he had encountered, Hinduism and Islam, he began new teachings that came to be known as Sikhism.

India's Mogul emperor, the great Akbar (ruled 1556–1605), deeply admired this new religion and gave land for its establishment. It was there that the foundation was laid for what came to be known as the city of Amritsar, literally the "Ocean of Immortality," where the famous Golden Temple was built. I participated in the celebration of the four hundredth anniversary of the compilation of the sacred Sikh scripture, the Adi Granth, which took place at the Golden Temple. The Sikhs deeply revere this scripture and recognize it as their final Guru. The story of how the tenth Guru, Gobind Singh, proclaimed that after him the sacred scripture, Adi Granth, would be the Guru of the Sikhs echoes a touching story from my own tradition. As the great eleventh-century Tibetan master Dromtönpa lay dying, with his head propped on the lap of his student Potowa, the tears of Potowa dropped onto the master's face. Drom looked up and asked "Why are you crying?" Potowa replied, "You are my Guru. Where will I find teaching now?" Drom said, "Do not fear. Take the scriptures as your Guru. You will find the teaching there."

My first visit to the Golden Temple took place on my first visit to India in 1956. Later, I had the honor of establishing a personal friendship with the noted Sikh teacher Sant Fateh Singh. Because he lived in Punjab, which is not too far from my own residence at Dharamsala, we were able to meet each other on a few occasions. Fateh Singh very kindly explained the history of the Sikh people to me, telling me the story of Guru Nanak and of the building of the Golden Temple. He invited me to participate in a formal ceremony of readings from the sacred Adi Granth and singing of hymns that the Sikhs call *bajans*, which are traditionally accompanied by a musical instrument rather like a harmonium. The degree to which the devout Sikhs venerate this scripture is most moving.

Inside their temple, which is known as the Guruduwara, there is a raised platform that is canopied. During prayers the scripture, which is wrapped inside silk brocade, is brought out and laid inside this canopied structure on a small stand. A master then reads from the scripture while someone waves a white fan next to it. Most of the time, the reading is done in the style of a chanted song accompanied with music. So it was wonderfully satisfying when I was invited by Punjab University at Patiala to unveil the English translation of this sacred scripture when the university formally launched it in 1992. Like many people of other faiths, I now had the opportunity to read the scripture and benefit from its spiritual wisdom.

One of the most admirable aspects of Sikh religious practice is its emphasis on service, especially to the poor. I have been to a number of Sikh Guruduwaras, including the famous one in Delhi. In most of these Sikh temples there are open kitchens where free meals are served to whoever happens to come by. Historically, this custom may have evolved from the need for compassionate service to the needy, such as offering hospitality to those weary on the road, the poor, and so on. I was told that it is customary for most Sikhs, even busy professionals in the cities, to work regularly at these open kitchens and help serve food. In fact, there is a beautiful verse in the Adi Granth:

Without selfless service, no objectives are fulfilled;
In service lies the purest action.

(GURU NANAK DEV, PAGE 992, LINE 7)

India as a Host to Other World Religions

Of the Abrahamic religions, probably the first one to appear on the Indian subcontinent is Christianity, something surprisingly not well-known. According to some historians, Saint Thomas, one of Jesus' own disciples, arrived on the shores of Kerala, near Cochin, in the first century CE, and he established churches in different parts of this southern Indian kingdom. I have, in fact, visited the church where Saint Thomas' tomb is venerated. Kerala also saw the arrival of one of the first communities of Jews in India, who arrived by boat over two thousand years ago and sought asylum in Cochin. I had the opportunity to visit an old Jewish synagogue that still stands in Kerala, with a small community of practicing Jews who represent the descendants of those early immigrants. Third came Islam, initially from the central Asian steppes, whose heirs later established the Mogul dynasty in India. The arrival of two other religions also had a lasting impact on the spiritual and religious landscape of India. They are Zoroastrianism, one of the oldest monotheistic religions, and the newer nineteenth-century religious movement known as the Bahá'i faith.

Born in Persia more than a thousand years before the Common Era, Zoroastrianism developed the monotheistic idea of a single, un-created God that is the source of all things. Today, one of the largest Zoroastrian communities lives in the Indian metropolis of Mumbai. One practice that we Tibetans share with the Zoroastrians is the custom of disposing of the dead by giving the body to the vultures as an act of charity. Members of this Indian community, often known as Parsees, are highly active in social service and charity work, especially in their establishment of hospitals and schools for the poor. Despite their long exile from their religious homeland, and the fact that they remain quite a small community—just over a hundred thousand—I find hugely admirable the way the Parsees have preserved their religious and cultural identity, as well as making a significant contribution to Indian society more widely.

The Bahá'i faith also has a substantial presence in India. Like Zoroastrianism, Bahá'ism was born in Persia. Founded by Bahá'u'lláh in the mid-nineteenth century, this highly syncretistic faith teaches that there is only one God, that all of the world's religions are from this one God, and that the time has arrived for humanity to recognize its oneness. Although I am not myself an advocate of religious syncretism, or the merging of distinct faiths, I have much admiration for the commitment of the Bahá'is to world peace. They pay special attention to overcoming prejudice—religious, cultural, racial, and gender-based—and claim that the search for genuine world peace is the crying need of our time. As a result, Bahá'is are particularly active in peace movements, attracting participation especially from among the young. They are also most visibly present in almost all inter-religious services.

I have had the honor to visit and pray inside the beautiful Bahá'i temple in New Delhi, which is shaped like a lotus flower with many petals. Today, this temple has become an architectural landmark in the Indian capital. During my first visit to the Middle East, in 1993, I was able to pay homage at the tomb of Bahá'u'lláh by visiting the spectacular shrine on Mount Carmel, in the Israeli port city of Haifa.

What the World Can Learn from India's Experience

One of the great facts of India's multireligious history is the near absence of any explicitly inter-religious wars over several millennia. India's first emperor, Ashoka, in the aftermath of his famous conquest of Kalinga, embraced Buddhism as his personal faith, but he ensured that the state itself remained fully tolerant of India's three great religions of the time—Buddhism, Hinduism, and Jainism. His court as well as his immediate ministers included members from all three great religions. The whole heritage of India's exemplary tolerance of religious diversity is encapsulated in Ashoka's twelfth rock edict, erected before the Common Era began:

> The Beloved of the Gods (the king) does not consider gifts or honor to be as important as the advancement of the essential doctrine of all sects. This progress of the essential doctrine takes many forms, but its basis is the control of one's speech so as not to extol one's own sect or disparage another's on unsuitable occasions, or at least to do so mildly on certain occasions. On each occasion one should honor another man's sect, for by doing so one increases the influence of one's own sect and benefits that of the other man; while by doing otherwise one diminishes the influence of one's own sect and harms the other man's. Again whosoever honors his own sect or disparages that of another man, wholly out of devotion to his own, with a view to showing it in a favorable light, harms his own sect even more seriously. Therefore, concord is to be commended, so that men may hear one another's principles. . . .
>
> (ASHOKA AND THE DECLINE OF THE MAURYAS, APPENDIX V)

During the medieval period, through successive dynasties and in the numerous separate kingdoms that constituted the Indian subcontinent, almost all rulers respected the beliefs of the three religions native to the land. Not only was the fact of their existence taken for granted but there was a most healthy intellectual competition and mutually respectful relations between the traditions. There was tremendous debate among the thinkers of the three traditions, each critiquing the standpoints of the others and each refining his own views in light of the others' critiques. Sometimes these debates got carried away, so that more than the defense of specific philosophical standpoints was at stake. It is said, for example, that occasionally there were formal public debates in the presence of the ruling king, where at the end the leader of the losing side, along with his immediate disciples, joined the tradition represented by the winning side. For example, the famous Buddhist monastery of Nalanda is said to have guarded each of its four main entrances with an expert debater. If an opponent approached the monastery, he would first have to prove himself worthy by debating the scholar-monk guarding that entrance! The result of this tradition of philosophical debate between religions is not only mutual enrichment of all three but also the flowering of a rich philosophical culture that is not divorced from a spiritual quest.

Recently, in a conversation, the noted Indian politician L.K. Advani pointed out to me that this long historical legacy of debates across diverse traditions is one of the key reasons why multiparty democracy came to be so firmly established in India. Furthermore, through these debates a culture was created whereby although individuals and groups engage in often passionate and heated debates, the parties still retain their respect for one another as serious and profound thinkers. In other words, a clear distinction is drawn between attacking the views and positions and the person who espouses and propounds those views. One clear example is the treatment of the so-called Materialist School known in Sanskrit as Carvaka. This is a school that propounded a philosophical view totally at odds with most of the mainstream classical Indian traditions. For example, unlike other schools the Carvakas reject any notion of a life after death and argue that when one meets with the physical end at death this is also the end of the existence of the individual as well. So they reject the concept of *karma* across lifetimes, as well as denying the existence of any transcendent creator. Furthermore, they reject the notion of any spiritual being; for the Carvakas existence equals material existence. So it is not surprising that all the other classical Indian schools critiqued this philosophy vehemently, accusing it to be a form of nihilism. Despite this, the original masters of this school were referred to with the respectful epithet *rishi*, which can be translated as "sages."

On the most mundane level, the presence of a family or an individual following a different religion living just next door—a phenomenon that is quite new to many regions of the world today—has been an everyday reality for more than two thousand years in India. That the family living next to one's own home does not follow the same religion as oneself was never seen as a threat to one's security or the validity of one's own faith tradition. On the whole, there was no impetus on the part of followers of each of the three religions to convert others—nor was there an urge to make one's own tradition the dominant faith.

Into this environment Islam arrived sometime after the tenth century CE. Although initially India's encounter with Islam came via sporadic raids carried out by hordes of central Asian nomads, whose primary aim was to loot the famed riches of the Indian temples, over time—through trade and the emergence of the Mogul kings—Islam became established as an important religious presence in India. The more enlightened Mogul rulers adjusted to the religious culture of India and embraced the longstanding ethos of pluralism and tolerance. Notable among these rulers was the Muslim emperor Akbar (1542–1605), who, like Ashoka, ruled with a policy of enlightened religious pluralism. Like Ashoka, he too employed Hindus and Jains in important positions in his government. He also abolished some of the discriminatory policies imposed by earlier Muslim rulers, such as the tax levied on non-Muslims.

Recognizing the historical legacy of religious pluralism and honoring the heritage of enlightened rulers like Ashoka and Akbar, India deliberately chose a secular constitution when it regained its Independence in 1947. By *secular* in this context what is meant is not a rejection of religion but, rather, a position equidistant from all faith traditions, including nonbelievers. India's secular constitution allows all religious traditions to flourish equally. I am aware that this is a different use of the term *secularism* from the way it is often understood in the West. In the latter case, the terms *secularism* and *secularist* are often contrasted with *religion* and *religious,* and they acquire a flavor of active rejection of any religious viewpoint. For the sake of convenience, in this book I use the term *secular* in this Western sense, not in the sense which it is used in the Indian constitution.

The recent, twentieth-century history of India has included tragic communal violence defined along the Hindu-Muslim religious divide. This is a tragic development whose deeper roots and causes are hugely complex, but it has much to do with the emergence of identity politics in a postcolonial world. Even in the midst of the worst manifestations of this violence, we have witnessed, in the example of Mahatma Gandhi, how a deeply religious person can counter these divisive forces. Gandhi, assisted by Maulana Azad and Khan Abdul Gaffar Khan, two prominent Muslims active in the cause of Hindu-Muslim unity, performed the task of tens of thousands of soldiers in the massive city of Calcutta in attempting to maintain the peace between India's two main communities during the tragic partition of the subcontinent into India and Pakistan. I had the good fortune to have known Abdul Gaffar Khan, often referred to as the "Frontier Gandhi."

To me, the great lesson of India's history is that genuine religious pluralism and toleration are achievable and, indeed, have been a historical fact. This has been true in other contexts, too, such as in the rich flowering of Jewish, Christian, and Muslim cultures in medieval Spain and Sicily—but nowhere for as long a period and in such richness as in India. The question is what the world can learn from India's example. At present, we face the truly frightening risk of turning away from any openness and tolerance of differences.

In today's increasingly globalized world, with its interconnected economic and environmental challenges, as well as the increasing proximity of peoples and cultures, many factors exert a pressure that tests the limits of our capacity for acceptance of others. Here, India truly remains a model of pluralism and toleration, especially on the religious level, and is a society where despite deep faith in their own religious traditions, individuals do not feel the need to bring the followers of other faith traditions into their religious fold. India, with its long history of tolerant coexistence, is a beacon for the rest of the world. In fact, when it comes to the wider world I see my own work as being a humble messenger of India's ancient teachings on *ahimsa* (nonviolence) and tolerance of religious pluralism. I see my efforts in promoting peace, nonviolent approaches to resolving conflicts, and understanding across boundaries of race, religion, and nations, all having their roots in the ancient Indian teachings. So, in every sense of the word, I remain truly a *chela* (disciple) of India.

3

HINDUISM:

ON THE BANKS

OF THE GANGES

The World's Largest Religious Gathering

When trying to understand the enduring power of Hinduism to inspire millions over many centuries, the religious gathering called the Great Kumbh Mela is a good place to start. This festival brings millions of devout Hindus together once every twelve years to celebrate their faith at the confluence of three sacred rivers—the Ganges, Yamuna, and Sarasvati, the last thought to have dried up about three thousand years ago. People come from all parts of India, from the foothills of the Himalayas to the furthermost edges of the south. They encompass all walks of life, from ascetic *sadhus* (holy men) to farmers in small villages, to modern educated people from the business and professional world. All are united by their devotion to the celebration of the sacred.

    I first had the privilege of participating in the Great Kumbh

Mela in 1977. Later I learned that several million pilgrims had gathered that year for the festival. For a non-Hindu, to be invited as a fellow pilgrim to this great religious gathering was truly an honor. To see and feel the immense collective devotion of the pilgrims was awe-inspiring; it was also an opportunity to glimpse the timeless dimension of India's ancient religious civilization. I reflected that, throughout time, ever since recorded history began in this great land of India, the Ganges has provided so much spiritual solace, peace, and comfort—as well as material sustenance through irrigating the fields—for millions of human beings that I, too, paid my deep homage to the river and prayed on its banks.

The origins of this amazing mass pilgrimage are deeply rooted in India's ancient spiritual heritage. Some say that the custom goes back four thousand years, to the age of the ancient Vedas, the sacred texts that are the earliest scriptures of the Hindus. That it is ancient is beyond doubt. The seventh-century Chinese Buddhist pilgrim Xuán Zàng provides an eyewitness account of the Kumbh Mela celebration. According to him, the pilgrims bathe in the Ganges, listen to sermons on the sacred scriptures from holy men, and pay respect to the *sadhus,* some of whom display great feats of asceticism. All these religious activities are integral to the pilgrimage and are aimed at purifying the souls of the participants from negative karma. The Ganges, which the Indians affectionately refer to as "Ganga Mata" (Mother Ganges), is most revered for its cleansing power. A devout Hindu will not only wish physically to touch and bathe in the river once in his or her lifetime but will hope to have his or her body cremated on the banks of the river and the ashes thrown into it.

The story of the mythic origin of the Ganges is quite familiar to classically educated Tibetans, as it figures prominently in Sanskrit poetic literature. According to this legend, the Ganges was brought down to earth from the heavens by Bhagiratha, a descendant of an ancient ruler of the Ayodhya kingdom, to help purify the ashes of his ancestors who had inadvertently offended a sage. On occasions I have attended the formal evening ceremony called Ganga Arti (worship of the Ganges), which is performed every night on the banks of the river in the holy city of Varanasi. The ritual consists of rites, performed by Brahmin priests, and includes a wide variety of offerings to the Ganges as well as the singing of hymns to the river goddess. The offerings—flowers, lamps, incense, perfume, and so on—are accompanied by the ringing of bells and the blowing of conches, and elegant hand gestures called *mudras*. These rites and the way they are conducted are strikingly similar to my own Tibetan Buddhist rituals. One feels a sense of timelessness in their presence, and the first time I attended this ceremony, the thought that this Ganga Arti celebration has been happening on this same riverbank for some three millennia filled me with a sense of awe. I was deeply honored when, with Shankar Acharya of Puri, I was actually allowed to participate in performing the rites—lifting the sacred flame, offering the incense, and sprinkling flowers.

During my first visit to the Great Kumbh Mela, I met with some of Hinduism's great spiritual leaders, especially the Shankar Acharyas, the four guardians of the Hindu faith. I had a special affinity with Shankar Acharya of Kanci, His Holiness Swami Dayendra, and I also struck an immediate rapport with Shankar Acharya of Puri, who is much younger than me and is deeply committed to promoting inter-religious harmony and understanding. Later on I was able to visit Shankar Acharya Dayendra's ashram in Kanci, in southern India.

Twenty-four years later, in 2001, barely a year after the advent of the new millennium of the Common Era, I had the honor once again to participate in the Great Kumbh Mela. This time, according to the news reports, some 70 million pilgrims gathered. During the entire festival—which lasted many days with so many people—all the catering was entirely vegetarian; not a single animal lost its life to feed human beings! In addition to the Shankar Acharyas, I met with numerous Jagath Gurus—important teachers of the Hindu faith from different parts of the country. At this Kumbh Mela celebration, not only did I take part in the prayers and rituals but I also partici- pated in a conference on relations between the religions, including the question of conversion in the new millennium, which resulted in the adoption of a joint declaration. In fact, one of the Jagath Gurus held my hand, looked deeply into my eyes, and expressed his per- sonal appreciation for my work in inter-religious understanding. This gesture was deeply encouraging to me.

What Is Hinduism?

As scholars of religion have pointed out, the word *Hinduism* is a somewhat problematic modern coinage. It covers a vast and wonder- fully diverse religious heritage, reaching back at least three millennia on the Indian subcontinent. Any term that attempts to characterize the variety of phenomena covered by this range is bound to simplify it. In classical Buddhist and Tibetan texts, a generic term *tirthika*, or its Tibetan equivalent *mutekpa* (literally "one who holds up a crossing to freedom"), is used to refer to the followers of all non-Buddhist In- dian schools, which includes Jainism and the six philosophical schools of the Vedic tradition. It is this usage I was familiar with in Tibet; however, not only external scholarship employs the term

Hinduism as a convenient catch-all. It has also become accepted in recent years as a general self-description for scholars and practitioners within India. Therefore, in this book, I shall follow current convention.

When thinking about Hinduism, it is helpful not to get bogged down by too many of the standard assumptions one makes about religion. There is no founder as such, nor is there any closed scriptural canon such as the Bible for Jews and Christians and the Qur'an for Muslims. Like Buddhism, Hinduism is not a "religion of the book." This is not to say that there are no holy scriptures sacred to the tradition. For example, the ancient Vedas are perceived by many Hindus as being utterances directly from God, with no human mediation. Similarly, the famed Bhagavad Gita is recognized as the divine words of Lord Krishna. Hinduism has many sages, but no founding historical figures like its religious siblings on the Indian continent, namely Buddhism and Jainism. On the doctrinal level, too, it is a truly pluralistic faith where conceptions of the ultimate truth—the Divinity—include views that are contradictory among the various schools. For example, some understand the Godhead in dualistic terms while others are categorically nondualistic.

Also, in people's expressions of devotion to manifestations of the Godhead, there are a wide range of approaches, each emphasizing a particular manifestation. For example, for many Lord Shiva is the central object of their worship, and he embodies the Godhead not only in its manifestation as the *creator* and progenitor of the world but also as the *preserver* and the final *destroyer* of all things. Some see these three acts—of creating, sustaining, and destroying—in terms of separate manifestations as Brahma, Vishnu, and Shiva, respectively. The remarkable thing about what one might call Hindu theology—the rational discourse pertaining to the Godhead—is its vast diversity and its intimations of the utter mystery of existence.

Hinduism teaches that human beings are subject to a series of goals in life. On the whole, we are pleasure-seeking creatures and seeking the fulfillment of this desire remains our nature at the basic level. However, we also seek worldly success in terms of wealth, fame, and power, and many see these pursuits as constituting the primary goals of life. If we stay on either of these two levels, Hinduism reminds us, we remain only on the path of desire. The potential of human life is greater than the achievement of worldly success and gratification of the senses. In fact, truly to live out the potential of a human life, we must transcend the path of desire and move beyond it to a path of renunciation. This is referred to as the Dharma, the way of the truth.

The suggestion is that any reflective human being, if he or she deeply contemplates the meaning of existence, will come to recognize that the quest for truth lies at the heart of human life. This quest for truth—the third goal—must remain an abiding aspiration for a human being. The final goal is true freedom, *moksha*, which is a freedom at the level of the spirit. The attainment of *moksha* constitutes for Hinduism the fulfillment of the purpose of human existence. In doing so, as it were, one has come full circle to where, transcending the narrowness of discreet individual existence, one has actualized the totality of reality, a state where the individual becomes one with the reality itself. Thus, the four goals of human life, according to Hinduism, are desire *(kama)*, worldly success *(artha)*, truth *(dharma)*, and spiritual freedom *(moksha)*; of these, the first two constitute the path of desire, the second two constitute the path of renunciation.

Interestingly, Buddhism shares a similar view about the four aims of human life. They are, however, presented in a slightly different way. One speaks of what are called the "four factors of perfection in life." These are presented within the framework of two sets of cause and effect, one pertaining to worldly aspiration and the other pertaining to transcendence from the world—somewhat akin to Hinduism's distinction between the paths of desire and renunciation. So *wealth,* or worldly success, and *desire* are paired as part of one causal network where wealth is the cause or the means while the fulfillment of desire constitutes its fruit or result. Similarly, *dharma* is the cause, or the means, while *moksha,* or spiritual freedom, is its fruit. This is an example of the way in which a later tradition (in this case, Buddhism) incorporates numerous elements such as ideas, insights, and practices that it inherits from the earlier tradition (in this case Hinduism).

Four Ways of Approaching the Godhead

As I live in India I have had the privilege of meeting numerous Hindu religious leaders and practitioners. One contemporary Hindu religious community that is most active internationally is the Brahmakumari order. With their headquarters in Mount Abu in Rajasthan, theirs is a celibate order of women who dress in white and are dedicated to a life of spiritual practice. Because of their commitment to inter-religious dialogue and harmony, I have had quite a lot of contact with this sisters' order and have indeed been to Mount Abu.

Among the Hindu religious leaders, a close neighbor was the late Swami Chinmayananda, whose main ashram is not far from Dharamsala. On a few occasions I visited his ashram and spent some time with him. From him, from the Brahmakumaris, and other teachers including Swami Vaswani, whose ashram in Pune I have visited, I learned much about the actual practice of the Hindu faith.

Hinduism propounds different ways of approaching the ultimate truth, which from the Hindu theological point of view can be equated with the Godhead.

There is, for example, "the way of the knowledge" *(jnana yoga)* that emphasizes the path to achieve oneness with God through knowledge. *Knowledge* here should not be understood in terms of intellectual, discursive knowledge of facts; rather, it is the knowledge of one's own nature—self-knowledge in the true sense of the word. A key element of this is to gain insight into the truth that one's own sense of self as a discrete, individuated ego is an illusion and that underlying this surface, everyday level of selfhood is a true Self. This is called *atman,* which is the God within, and unlike our temporal, individuated self, it is eternal, unitary, and independent. Through learning the scriptures, through critically reflecting upon the truth of *atman,* and through internalizing the path by way of meditation, the seeker of truth comes to actualize this profound knowledge. Following the Upanishads, a set of early Hindu scriptures, the approach of knowledge toward understanding the nature of self as well as God came to occupy a prominent position in the Hindu tradition. In fact, the six classical Hindu schools of philosophy known as the six *darshanas*—Samkhya and Yoga, Vaisheshika and Nyaya, Mimamsa and Vedanta—can all be seen as developments of *jnana yoga.* Given the tremendous influence of the eighth-century Hindu sage Adi Shankara, over time, the Vedanta school and its interpretation of the holy scriptures came to define what could be called Hindu theology and philosophy.

Another way to God is through *bhakti yoga,* which primarily emphasizes single-pointed devotion to the love of God. Unlike the way of knowledge, this second approach requires attributing personal qualities to the Godhead so that the devotee can experience a sense of intimacy with God, almost in the manner of a deep friendship. Here, Hinduism, with its myths, its great pantheon of divinities, and its rituals and chanting, displays a tremendous richness. A true practitioner of *bhakti* is able to totally submit the personal ego and offer his or her entire being to the love of God, such that the transcendence of ego boundaries occurs naturally in the act of deep devotion.

This passionate love of God is often expressed by the religious person in the form of poetry. One of the most popular poets in this tradition was the sixteenth-century woman mystic Mirabai, whose love of Lord Krishna is legendary:

MIRABAI HAS FINISHED WITH WAITING

O friends on this path,
My eyes are no longer my eyes.
A sweetness has entered through them,
Has pierced through to my heart.
How long did I stand in the house of this body
And stare at the road?
My Beloved is a steeped herb, he has cured me for life.
Mira belongs to Giridhara, the One Who Lifts All,
And everyone says she is mad.

(MIRABAI: ECSTATIC POEMS)

The practice of *bhakti* may involve, among other things, the constant invocation of God's name— "*Jai Rama, Jai Rama*" being a popular example—and the singing of hymns and chanting of praises to the Lord. To this day, this *bhakti* tradition remains extremely strong among the Hindus in India.

A third way to God, known as *karma yoga*, emphasizes the approach of actual work in the form of service. Here, in living out one's everyday life and devoting oneself whole-heartedly to one's work, one cultivates the truth of God. Whether it is bringing up your children, or teaching in a school, or working in a corporate office, if people are able to bring the awareness of God into their work they are approaching the truth of the Godhead. The key here is to engage with one's work in a way that transcends the concerns of narrow ego-centeredness.

Finally there is the way of *raja yoga*, or the royal way to God. This involves profound contemplative exercises that integrate physical exercises with psychological approaches, such as single-pointed concentration and visualization. The aim here is to arrive at the state where the duality of subject and object is totally dissolved, and to abide in this state totally beyond the dichotomies of thought and time. Many of the key elements of *raja yoga* practice are, at least in form, common to meditation practices found in my own Buddhist tradition. Whether it is in adopting an appropriate sitting posture, called *asana,* or watching one's breath, called *pranayama*—which are, in a sense, preliminary stages to deeper inner concentration such as *samadhi*—the forms and methods are similar. On a still deeper level, just as one finds more esoteric teachings called *tantra* in the Buddhist tradition, which involve the full range of subtle and sensual energies in the body, so parallel teachings on *tantra* appear in the Hindu tradition. Within the fourfold approach to God in Hinduism, these *tantric* practices can be seen as part of *raja yoga.*

The interesting thing about these four paths is that, although they are presented as alternative ways of experiencing God, for most practitioners the most effective approach includes elements from all four ways. Generally, the first approach—the way of knowledge—is most suited to people of a philosophical bent of mind; the second, the way of devotion or *bhakti,* is suited to those with a more devotional disposition; the way of work is for those with an active personality; and finally, *raja yoga*, is recommended for those with a more contemplative and yogic disposition.

Seeing the Divine in Diverse Forms

Perhaps the most admirable quality of Hinduism, at least to me, is its lack of dogmatism when it comes to the conception of the Godhead, the Highest Truth. Historically, despite the differences of sects—such as the Shaivites, who worship God in the form of Lord Shiva, and the Vishnuites, who prioritize Vishnu—on the theological and philosophical levels Hinduism has remained open. This openness at the heart of Hinduism makes it possible for eminent Hindu teachers to state that the various religions are different languages through which God speaks to the human heart. For Hinduism, this openness to other religions is by no means a newly acquired sensibility. For example, in the ancient scriptures called the Puranas (Origin Stories), which tell of the various reincarnations of Vishnu in the world of humans, the historical Buddha—the founder of Buddhism—is described as one such incarnation *(avatar)*.

This celebration of religious diversity—alongside of toleration and pluralism—remained prominent in India during the nineteenth century, thanks primarily to the great contributions of the Hindu saints Swami Ramakrishna and Vivekananda. Fully to understand and taste the beauty of other faith traditions, it is said, Ramakrishna even engaged in deeds that may have been quite offensive to the religious sensibilities of his more orthodox fellow Hindus. He composed Christian *sadhanas* (meditations on God), participated in Friday *namaz* (worship) in mosques. In his own personal spirituality, Ramakrishna reached a high level of attainment. Ramakrishna and his order represent a remarkable and profound modern example of true ecumenism and deep inter-religious exploration. I find their model consistently inspiring, especially since it proceeds from a wellspring of genuine spiritual experience.

Ramakrishna's principal student Swami Vivekananda was an active participant in the ecumenical movement that included the first conference of the World Parliament of Religions in Chicago in 1893, as the nineteenth century was drawing to a close. There, Vivekananda spoke of how the time had come for all religions of the world to recognize each other as valid paths to the Ultimate Truth, and he called on them to avoid imposing their own versions of the truth upon others. Citing a hymn, Vivekananda spoke of how the different religions can be seen as different streams, each flowing through different terrain and yet ultimately all converging in the great ocean. Having been an admirer of the vision behind the World Parliament of Religions—note the two key words *parliament,* which suggests a democratic principle, and *religions,* which is in the plural— it was wonderful for me to participate in 1992 in the hundredth anniversary of Vivekananda's 1892 pilgrimage to Kanyakumari, which he undertook before his journey to Chicago.

I have had a close friendship with one of the twentieth-century's greatest representatives of the Ramakrishna mission, my friend the late Swami Ranganathananda. In 1986, at Swamiji's invitation, I visited Vivekananda's monastic community in Hyderabad, in southern India, where I shared a meal with the monks and engaged in a dialogue with them. It was then that I learned how Vivekananda had modeled his monastic order on the Buddha's monastic community, the *sangha.* In fact, the image of the Buddha was an important presence at this monastery. One particularly admirable aspect of the Ramakrishna mission is its deep commitment to social service, especially in the areas of education and health. One finds schools and hospitals funded and administered by this mission all over India. In fact, there are many examples throughout India of religious communities engaged in active social service out of compassionate concern for the poor and the needy.

Once Swamiji and I shared a platform in Calcutta, discussing the interface between science and spirituality at a dialogue moderated by my longtime friend Rajiv Mehrotra, a noted media figure in India. At that meeting, Swamiji made the point that, when speaking of science and spirituality, it is critical to take into account the cultural and historical contexts. Since there has never been a divide between the spiritual and the material in India, as there has been in the West, Swamiji suggested that the relationship between science and spirituality is bound to have a different flavor in the Indian context. Swamiji also spoke of God in the form of a depth dimension of the human personality and said that one could discover God in every human being. According to him, what religions call "God" is not something sitting in the sky far away but is present in each of us. This, Swamiji argued, is a great discovery of India's ancient culture.

Swamiji was a most gentle person; deeply spiritual, he was also tremendously articulate in English. Having never quite mastered the language myself—to this day I rely on the help of my translator—I felt much admiration for his facility with English. Being myself a great enthusiast for dialogue between science and spirituality, and a proponent of inter-religious understanding through dialogue, I felt a strong affinity with him. In the aftermath of the demolition of the mosque in Ayodhya and the communal clashes it gave rise to, Swamiji worked tirelessly to diffuse the tension and appealed strongly for saner heads to prevail in both Hindu and Muslim communities in India. This was a great contribution at a difficult time.

Hindu-Buddhist Dialogue, a Historical Aside

Historically, Hinduism and Buddhism have had an extremely long relationship. From competing for the patronage of the early rulers of the various kingdoms in India to mutual intellectual enrichment through debate and philosophical discourse, from sharing an artistic and architectural heritage to the inheritance of the great spiritual and philosophical ideas of karma and reincarnation, from the shared use and development of Sanskrit as the key medium of scriptural discussion to the exploration of esoteric yogic practices, numerous things bind these two Indian religions. There is a great commonality of spiritual practices between Hinduism and Buddhism, from meditations on stilling the mind to the application of antidotes to the afflictions, from *tantric* visualization practices to a multiplicity of breath-based spiritual exercises. The area where the cross-fertilization of ideas between these two traditions has been most fruitful is in the domain of philosophical thought, especially in epistemology, or the theory of knowledge.

For example, the second-century Indian Buddhist thinker Nagarjuna drew extensively from the Hindu Nyaya tradition when he developed his critiques of the foundationalist theory of knowledge. Similarly, in the fifth century, Dignaga, effectively the father of Buddhist logic and epistemology, developed a sophisticated system of epistemology that involved a detailed critique of the Nyaya school of logic. Dignaga's school was developed further by Dharmakirti in the seventh century, whose position in turn was an object of sustained critique by Hindu thinkers, such as Uddyotakara and Kumarila Bhatta. In the eighth century, Shantarakshita—one of the earliest Indian Buddhist philosophers to come to my own country, Tibet—responded to Kumarila Bhatta's critiques and refined Dharmakirti's epistemological ideas in the light of Hindu critiques. Other Indian schools that debated logic and epistemology include Vaishashika and Purvamimamsa. The end result of all of these debates has been a refinement of the standpoints of the respective schools and the flowering of a highly sophisticated philosophical heritage on the Indian subcontinent. A central focus of philosophical inquiry across all schools in classical India has been the questions pertaining to the nature of the mind, its relationship with the external world, and the complex web of thoughts, emotions, and habits that make up our mental world.

Alongside these philosophical explorations of the mind and its functions, the Indian traditions have also developed sophisticated mental-training practices to help cultivate and develop specific qualities of the mind. I hope that, as modern science advances in its understanding of the mind and its underlying brain mechanisms, a fruitful dialogue may emerge whereby the insights of the Indian philosophies could be interfaced with those of scientific inquiry. I have had the fortune to initiate a series of conversations between experts in classical Indian thought, including Tibetan Buddhist scholars, on various questions of philosophical interest. These conversations, which were held at the Central Tibetan University in Sarnath, Varanasi, were most stimulating and demonstrated the richness of the classical Indian philosophical heritage. Within this, heritage it is the classical Indian Buddhist heritage that we Tibetans inherited, and of it we have become its custodians, especially after the demise of Buddhism in its own birthplace in India.

The Place of Compassion

The centrality of selfless compassion as the motivation for human action in the world is enshrined in the Dharmasutra of Gautama, one of the most influential Brahmanic law codes, dating back possibly to as early as the third century BCE, where "compassion for all creatures" is the first of the eight virtues of the self (8:22–3). The idea is beautifully presented in some of the greatest Hindu sacred texts. Perhaps the most beloved of these scriptures is the famous Bhagavad Gita, which presents a series of spiritual teachings given by Lord Krishna to the hero Arjuna. In the course of these teachings, Krishna preaches the virtue of selfless action for the benefit of the world: "Looking only to what maintains the world, you too must act" (Bhagavad Gita 3:20).

The sense of a universal welfare for all beings—the heart of compassion—is enjoined on Arjuna as the mark of the enlightened person:

> Seers whose impurities have been destroyed, whose doubts have been dispelled, who have restrained themselves, who delight in the welfare of all beings, reach the nirvana of Brahman.
>
> (BHAGAVAD GITA 5:25)

More than once, compassion is listed in the Gita as one of the qualities of the enlightened being—"without hatred for any creature, friendly and compassionate, free from possessiveness and egoism" (Gita 12:13). Krishna's instructions to Arjuna take the form of drawing his attention to the limitations of self-centered concerns. For when your action is guided by such considerations, given the narrowness of the confines of an egoistic self, the deed can never be truly expansive. However, once you can transcend the limits of self-concern, infinite possibilities of working for the welfare of the world open up in a being whose spirit is touched by "non-violence, truth-fulness, freedom from anger, absence of calumny, compassion for creatures, freedom from greed, modesty, steadiness" (Gita 16:2).

Other Hindu scriptures also emphasize the centrality of compassion. For instance, in the Shiva Mahapurana, one of the great Shaivite texts, it is written: "There is no other dharma better than to extend compassion to all beings. Therefore all the people should extend compassion to all creatures" (Rudra Samhita, chap. 5).

In the end, what is most compelling are the personal examples of individuals who exemplify the apogee of what is possible in a faith tradition. When I think of Hinduism, I think of great beings like Mahatma Gandhi, Vinoba Bhave, Baba Amte, and their like. Hinduism was the bedrock of inspiration and strength for Gandhi on his life's journey of bringing freedom to his people. It was Hinduism where he sought his personal solace, and it was in the language of Hinduism that he would experience the Divine within. Vinoba Ji (1895–1982), a contemporary of Gandhi, was also a great freedom fighter. In independent India, he worked tirelessly to redress social injustice and was instrumental in the redistribution of agricultural land so that families that had traditionally worked the land as bonded tenants became its owners. This is truly spiritual work, *dharma* work, with far-reaching consequences for the lives of many millions who happened to be born into unfortunate circumstances.

I was a great admirer of Baba Amte (1914–2008). He took upon his shoulders the responsibility for looking after a group of human beings shunned by the majority—the lepers. Baba established a colony for lepers in Warora in Maharashtra state, not too far from a Tibetan agricultural settlement. Baba did not simply feed and provide shelter for sufferers of leprosy, but he also helped restore their dignity, especially through work and the learning of new skills. His colony taught them how to make various artifacts, creating a real sense of community and providing an environment where lepers could live as normal human beings. Baba's story reminded me of a Tibetan saint named Dromtönpa, who dedicated the latter part of his life to serving lepers in central Tibet, eventually himself falling victim to the disease. For a long time, I wanted to make a substantial contribution to Baba's work but never quite had the funds to do this. But when I was awarded the Nobel Peace Prize in 1989 and learned of the substantial check that comes with it, I was so pleased to make a donation to Baba's colony.

Within a few months of receiving the award, I was able to visit Baba's leprosy colony once again. When Baba thanked me for my gift, I told him that it was actually I who should thank him. I said, "I only teach others about compassion and altruism. You, on the other hand, are doing it." Later in life, Baba also became one of the strongest Indian voices on the environment, embarking on a long march even in his old age to protest the building of a dam on the Narmada River. With his death in February 2008, the world lost a truly powerful symbol of humanity, justice, and compassion. For myself, I lost a close friend and a powerful source of personal inspiration.

4

CHRIST

AND THE

BODHISATTVA IDEAL

Jesus and the Compassionate Ideal

To a Buddhist like me, brought up all my life to uphold the ideal of compassion as the highest possible spiritual value, the image of Jesus on the Cross—taking on himself the suffering of all beings—is deeply inspiring. Such self-sacrifice, born out of altruism and universal love for all beings, is a perfect example of what Buddhists might term the Bodhisattva ideal. This concept of taking upon oneself the suffering of others is actually very much part of my own daily spiritual practice. In the Tibetan tradition, there is a popular meditation known as *tonglen,* literally "giving and taking," that involves imagining taking on the pain and suffering of others, as well as the causes of that suffering, while passing on to them one's own happiness and good fortune.

Beside this great symbol of compassion, Christianity offers also an incredibly intimate and moving symbol of love, in the image of Mary holding the baby Jesus. This links up with the deep meaning of motherhood as the ground for compassion, and it evokes the universal human need for love and affection. Thus, in addition to the utterly uncompromising resolve even to die a terrible death for the sake of human beings, which we find in the Crucifixion, Christianity emphasizes the simple and familiar love of mother and child. Yet the one is rooted in the other, and the compassion signaled by both is proclaimed as an accessible possibility for all human beings. This is a beautiful teaching—and one very close to my own Buddhist tradition, which compares loving-kindness and compassion with the unconditional affection of a mother for her children and then extends that affection until it encompasses all beings.

I had come across the symbol of the cross in Tibet when I was a child. It was on the cover of a Tibetan version of the Bible, which had been translated shortly after I was born. It was a thick book in a broad, handwritten script that had been printed in stencil through Cyclostyle duplication. Later I also saw the image of Jesus on the cross. At that time there was a Tibetan-speaking Kinnauri (from northern India) called Tharchin Babu, who had converted to Christianity and produced a regular newsletter called "Mirror of News," which was the only newspaper printed in Tibetan. Produced in Kalimpong, just across the Indian border, this was eagerly awaited by many people including me, as it was one of the best windows onto the outside world. It turns out that, for Tharchin, a devout Christian, the production of this newsletter was an act of service to the Tibetan people. After my escape to India, I had the chance to meet him and thank him for his kindness.

The first person to bring Christianity really to life for me was the late American Trappist monk Thomas Merton. In fact, one of the key themes Merton and I discussed at our meeting in 1968, when he visited me in northern India, was the centrality of the compassionate ideal of relieving others from suffering as a key motivation in both Buddhism and Christianity. So, right from the start, for me it was quite easy to find a deep resonance with the Christian symbol of the cross and the person of Jesus. In reading the Bible, I have been struck by how Jesus' miracles are so often motivated by compassion for the suffering of his fellow beings. His healings, his teachings, his miracle of the loaves and fishes all arise from a direct and immediate sense of compassion. Moreover, so much of his teaching emphasizes compassion. For example, in the Gospel according to Saint John, Jesus says "Greater love has no one than this, that he lay down his life for his friends" and again, "My command is this: Love each other" (John 15:12–18). In the famous Sermon on the Mount, which for me is one of the most beautiful teachings in the gospels, Jesus says: "You have heard that it was said, 'Love your neighbor and hate your enemy.' But I tell you: Love your enemies and pray for those who persecute you" (Matt. 5:43–4).

And it is striking, too, how the disciples who spread his teachings after Jesus's death did so by underlining that his compassion be emulated. A most touching passage, which has resonated in my mind since it was introduced to me, is from the First Letter of Paul to the Corinthians:

If I speak in the tongues of men and of angels, but have not love, I am only a resounding gong or a clanging cymbal. If I have the gift of prophecy and can fathom all mysteries and all knowledge, and if I have a faith that can move mountains, but have not love, I am nothing. If I give all I possess to the poor and surrender my body to the flames, but have not love, I gain nothing. Love is patient, love is kind. It does not envy, it does not boast, it is not proud. It is not rude, it is not self-seeking, it is not easily angered, it keeps no record of wrongs. Love does not delight in evil but rejoices with the truth. It always protects, always trusts, always hopes, always perseveres. Love never fails.

(I COR. 13:1–8)

This goes to the essence of things. All our views, opinions, hard-won principles are really quite worthless—however "right" they may be—if they are not driven by a compassionate motivation. However great our achievements or strenuous our actions, they are pointless if not rooted in that selfless compassion for other beings that Paul describes so well here. Once one grasps the centrality of the compassionate ideal in Christianity, then it is no wonder that Christianity has produced such models of altruism as Saint Francis of Assisi or the modern-day saint, Mother "Teresa" of Calcutta. Actually, the first time I heard someone read from the prayer believed by many to have been written by Saint Francis, I thought I was hearing a Christian practitioner reading from a Buddhist text, such as the writing of the eighth-century Buddhist teacher Shantideva.

To give a glimpse of the striking similarity between the aspiration prayers of these two spiritual teachers—each from a totally different faith tradition—I shall cite a few lines here. For example, Saint Francis prays:

Lord, make me an instrument of Thy peace;
where there is hatred, let me sow love;
where there is injury, pardon;

where there is doubt, faith;

where there is despair, hope;

where there is darkness, light;

and where there is sadness, joy.

O Divine Master,

grant that I may not so much seek to be consoled as to console;

to be understood, as to understand;

to be loved, as to love;

for it is in giving that we receive,

it is in pardoning that we are pardoned,

and it is in dying that we are born to Eternal Life.

In a similar vein, Shantideva makes this aspiration:

> May I be a protector for the unprotected;
> A guide for travelers on the way;
> A boat, a raft, or a bridge
> For those who long to cross to the other shore.
>
> May I be an isle for those who seek an island;
> A lamp for those who wish for light;
> A shelter for those in need of rest;
> A servant for those in need of service.
>
> (BODHICARYAVATARA 3:17–18)

I first visited Assisi in 1986, when the late pope, His Holiness John Paul II, who treated me over the many years we knew each other with the kindness of a father, called a world-religions summit there. Perhaps what I primarily learned from John Paul, who was the first pope to travel widely and become an international presence, was the impact for good that a leader of a world religion can have on the global stage. John Paul II was strikingly single-minded, and he confronted every major global issue with the inner conviction of his own Christian faith. The first pope I met, however, was his predecessor, His Holiness Pope Paul VI. This was in 1973, when I went to Rome for the first time. I felt rather humbled, confronted by the leader of so many millions of Roman Catholics all over the world, and the spiritual master of such inspiring figures as Desideri, Merton, and Mother Theresa.

That year, during an extensive visit to Europe, I also spent several days in London, where I first met the Reverend Edward Carpenter, the dean of Westminster Abbey, and his wife Lilian. Later, when I was able to return to Britain in 1979, I stayed as their guest at the Deanery, Westminster Abbey. We established a close bond, and in their presence I felt as if I were their son—indeed, I used to call Lilian "Mother." For me personally, the gentleness and warmth of the Carpenters was an ideal example of Christian love. It was Dean Carpenter who later introduced me to Robert Runcie, the former Archbishop of Canterbury, whose successors George Carey and Rowan Williams, I also count as spiritual colleagues.

My own encounter with Christian practitioners has impressed me strongly with the value of social activism—of the ways compassion must be put into the actual service of others, especially the weak and the vulnerable. I have always been touched by the dedication with which Christians, including missionaries, have gone to the remotest and the poorest places in the world, bringing education and health care. The Tibetans have also been beneficiaries of the charitable work of numerous Christian relief services, especially in the early years of our exile in India in the 1960s and '70s. Many of these Christian volunteers have come from the first world, leaving behind their life of relative comfort and ease, and have chosen to embrace a world of hardship and privation out of compassionate concern for others. The strong tradition of Christian values as a spur to helping others and improving the world—for instance, in the powerful Christian faith of the pioneers in the abolition of slavery in the eighteenth and nineteenth centuries, especially in the work of the Quakers and Anglican evangelists like William Wilberforce, or Martin Luther King Jr.'s extraordinary leadership in the American civil rights movement—remains hugely inspiring as a symbol of the good that religious faith can work in the world.

This was a topic I particularly discussed with Cardinal Basil Hume, who was for a long time the leader of Britain's Roman Catholics and with whom I had a particular rapport. Today, for example, Archbishop Desmond Tutu's work in the dissolution of apartheid, and especially in the healing work he undertook as chairman of the Truth and Reconciliation Commission, stands as a living testimony to the power and redeeming quality of religious service by a member of the cloth. I have known and appreciated Bishop Tutu as a friend and spiritual brother for more than two decades.

This active model of compassion within Christianity is one that I urge on my fellow Buddhist monks and nuns. I remember vividly a conversation I had in 1967 with the Supreme Patriarch of the Thai tradition, when I had the opportunity to make my first overseas trip from India. Inspired by the wonderful example of the Christian monks and nuns, I suggested to him that our Buddhist monks and nuns, too, should take a more active role in society, especially in the fields of education and health. The Most Venerable Elder's response was that the monastic precepts specifically command a life of separation from the laity, so it may not be appropriate for monks and nuns in the Buddhist tradition to take such a role in the world. This is true, but I felt then and feel to this day that since compassion is the central ideal in Buddhism, Buddhist monks and nuns should dedicate a significant part of their time and attention to service of this kind.

Monasticism in Buddhist and Christian Traditions

One thing that Buddhism and Christianity share is monasticism. Thomas Merton described to me the writings of John Cassian, one of the great monastic fathers of early Christianity who introduced the monastic way of life from Egypt to Western Europe in the fifth century. For Merton, Cassian was the great monastic writer of the Christian West. In his first *Conference,* Merton stressed, Cassian emphasized the cultivation of a pure heart as the grounds for ascent to the perfection of love. He stressed that the point of the various rigors of the monastic life is to keep the heart pure and unsullied by harmful passions.

According to the last chapter of the *Rule of Saint Benedict,* the most influential of the monastic rules of Western Christendom, which was codified in the sixth century, the point of monastic discipline is to make possible a blameless life that will lead to perfection. Many of the features that Saint Benedict stresses are similar to those codified in the Buddhist *vinaya* (the monastic discipline texts): Silence and the avoidance of loose talk, zeal, humility, obedience, patience. As with any ascetic community, the *Rule* sets out a series of social restrictions on the way a group striving for spiritual fulfillment should regulate itself, including matters of meals, daily work, special retreat conditions (such as in Lent), conduct outside the monastery, and so forth.

I gather there are some traditions, like that represented by Saint John Climacus, who was a monk at Sinai in the seventh century, that explicitly cast the restrictions of monasticism as a path to purification in ways closely parallel to how the path of Buddhism is traditionally presented. Climacus envisaged a "divine ladder" of thirty steps leading from the renunciation of a nonspiritual life through stages such as penitence, remembrance of death, mourning (many of which are actually meditation subjects in the Buddhist tradition), and the elimination of cankers like falsehood, slander, malice, and despondency to the final rungs of the ladder—"discernment," "stillness," "prayer," "dispassion," and finally "faith, hope and love."

This seems strikingly to confirm what Merton said when he wrote in his *Asian Journal:*

> Traditional monasticism faces the same problems of man and his happiness, what his life is for. . . . Buddhist and Christian monasticism start from the problem inside man himself. . . . Both Christianity and Buddhism agree that the root of man's problems is that his consciousness is all fouled up and he does not apprehend reality as it fully and really is.
>
> (PAGES 331–32)

And again:

> Consequently Christianity and Buddhism look primarily to a transformation of man's consciousness—a transformation, and a liberation of the truth imprisoned in man by ignorance and error.
>
> (PAGES 332–33)

When we met in November 1968, I pressed Merton about the vows of his Cistercian Order, and whether the vows meant that a monk was committed to strive for high spiritual attainment. I wanted to know if these vows constituted an initiation into a tradition of spiritual practice under a qualified master, analogous to the initiation by a Guru of a neophyte in the Buddhist Vajrayana tradition, or if they were more a social agreement "to stick around" (as Merton put it in his characteristically down-to-earth manner). I also wanted to know what kind of attainment Christian monks might achieve and if there were possibilities for a deep mystical life in the monasteries. Merton was wonderfully honest and said that was what they are supposed to be for, but that many monks seem to be interested in something else. Of course, what he said is true equally of Tibetan monasteries and of all traditions.

Yet, in the years after my meeting with Merton, during which I have had the chance to travel extensively and to see for myself what until the early 1970s I could only hear about, I have been deeply impressed by the sincerity of the Christian monastic tradition. I once visited a contemplative monastery in France and was profoundly touched by the simplicity of the lifestyle, and how the monks there live mostly in silence and in detachment from the world. The abbot and I remarked on the striking similarities in the discipline and the ethos that govern the life of contemplative monks in both traditions. I gather that, like Buddhism, Christianity has both an individual hermit tradition and a collective monastic lifestyle. In fact, in the Tibetan tradition, hermetic life is seen as the highest ideal. There is the expression "like a wounded animal in the wilderness" that captures the deep yearning of a monk to become a hermit and at the end of his life to wither away alone in the silence of the wild. Whenever I think of this expression it likewise exerts a powerful pull for me toward the hermetic life.

Divinity and Humanity

Given that Christianity is a major theistic religion, clearly central is the belief in God, the Supreme Being upon whom everything is dependent. It is the source, the final cause, and the reason for all things existent, yet is itself uncaused and not contingent upon anything else—in short, it is a necessary being. What makes the Christian vision of Divinity unique is the portrayal of God with a human face—namely, the person of Jesus. For Christianity, Jesus is not half human and half divine. Rather, he is fully human and fully divine; in other words, he is both God *and* man. This understanding of Divinity in human form brings the presence of God powerfully close to the human heart, adding an extraordinary dimension to the idea that humans are created in the image of God. The vision of Divinity immanent within humanity clearly creates a sense of intimacy with God in the hearts of Christian believers.

I remember vividly an exchange on the concept of God with the late Benedictine monk Father Bede Griffiths, who wore the saffron robes of an Indian holy man. Since Griffiths lived many years in India and was familiar with Buddhist and Hindu beliefs in relation to rebirth and previous lives, I once asked him: "For a Christian practitioner, what is wrong in accepting the theory of rebirth?" He said that belief in reincarnation would contradict the Christian understanding that this very life, one's particular life, is created by God. I was moved by the conviction and simplicity with which he said this. The power of this concept immediately struck me. I realized how meaningful it must be to understand that one's own life is created directly by God. This naturally affords a powerful sense of connection with God—in fact, a sense of intimacy almost in the fashion of a child's love toward its mother. Generally speaking, the closer you feel to someone, the likelier you will be to listen to his or her wishes, so the closeness of the relationship to God becomes the motivation for living a sound religious life.

After Griffiths's death, his work, and especially its focus of bringing contemplative practice back into Christian life, was followed for many years by Brother Wayne Teasdale, one of his principal disciples. Like his mentor, Teasdale wore a saffron habit and looked more like a Hindu holy man than a Catholic monk. (Brother Wayne initiated a series of interfaith conversations called Synthesis Dialogues that provided an excellent forum for genuine practitioners of different faiths to come together. It was actually at one of these Synthesis Dialogues that I met the Syrian thinker Jaoudat Mohamad, popularly known as Jawdat Said, with whom I felt immediate rapport.) Wayne's untimely death was a great loss.

For a Christian, the story of Jesus' death on the cross has a deep redeeming meaning and demonstrates God's concern for humanity. In suffering on the cross, God took upon himself all the ills of the world, thus effecting a profound reconciliation between humanity and himself. The idea that, in the person of Jesus, God helped atone for the sins of humanity exerts a powerful effect on the minds of the devout. It acts as a constant reminder of the need for a sense of gratitude to God and carries the moral responsibility to act in a way that expresses this gratitude. I can see how the idea of atonement can be a powerful motivating factor to live one's life according to the wishes of God. I was told that, in fact, the English word *atonement* is derived from the idea of "at-one-ment," suggesting a sense of unification and oneness. This is beautiful—it resonates with an aspiration that is quite common in the Tibetan tradition where, in the act of praying to the Buddha of Compassion, for example, one says, "Through this act may I be unified with you."

At the core of Catholic Christian theology lies the doctrine of the Holy Trinity. This is the teaching that God is one but is comprised of three aspects—the Father, the Son, and the Holy Spirit—who are not separate but dwell each in the other as a single substance. This has led to much complex theological discourse and numerous definitions, but the key point for me is that the very difficulty of this concept recognizes a profound mystery at the heart of reality. One might say that the Trinity is an emblem to contemplate the fundamental issues of the finite and the infinite, the temporal and the atemporal, the relative and the ultimate. The fact that the Second Person of the Trinity, Jesus the Son of God, possesses two natures—human and divine—is a way of reflecting on the perfectibility of humankind and the possibilities for salvation for all human beings.

Although, in the final analysis, the full nature of Divinity must remain beyond the boundaries of language and thought, there is perhaps a parallel between the concept of the Trinity and the Buddhist understanding of the threefold embodiment of Buddhahood, especially in the Sanskrit tradition—Dharmakaya, Sambhogakaya, and Nirmanakaya. In this theory, the true nature of final Buddhahood—the perfected state of our existence—is Dharmakaya, ultimate truth itself, which transcends time, space, and form. However, it is from this atemporal, infinite expanse and out of the Enlightened One's boundless compassion that the Buddha's embodiment spontaneously arises in the form of a subtle energy. This is referred to as the Sambhogakaya. One might see this as the intermediate stage between the utter formlessness of Buddha's essential reality of Dharmakaya and his full embodiment in the form of a physical, tangible being called Nirmanakaya, which literally means the Buddha body of perfect emanation. Incidentally, the historical Buddha Shakyamuni is understood to be an example of Nirmanakaya.

I am not suggesting here that these two doctrines—the Christian Holy Trinity and the Buddhist Trikaya theory (the Threefold

Embodiment of Buddhahood)—are somehow equivalent. The parallel I am drawing is in the paradox both of these doctrines seek to address, which is the relationship between time and timelessness, the finite and the infinite. Both traditions need a mediating force between the ultimate and the world of existence. I knew a Christian monk, Dom Sylvester Hovédard, from Prinknash Abbey in Britain, who explored the parallels between these doctrines. He was a great ecumenist, interested in Buddhist meditation practices, as well as a noted spiritual poet. I remember, once in our conversation, I drew Dom Sylvester's attention to the fact that, in the final analysis, despite the striking parallels between Buddhist and Christian doctrines, the two traditions have to part company when it comes to the notion of an absolute Transcendent Being. For Buddhism, given the centrality of an understanding of the universality of the law of causality and interdependence, from the philosophical point of view, any notion of the absolute is problematic.

One occasion that gave me a wonderful opportunity to delve deeply into the parallels between Christianity and Buddhism was the 1994 annual John Main Seminar that took place over three full days in London. This series of seminars is named after Father John Main, a Benedictine monk who had set up a Christian meditation group. I met him twice in the 1980s in Canada, and on the second occasion, I joined Main's community in a prayer session. They sang a hymn to guitar accompaniment, and as the hymn proceeded, John Main—with his eyes closed and deeply absorbed—had tears flowing down his cheeks. I was moved by the depth of his devotion and the inspirational power of a theistic belief to stir someone to such depths. In Tibetan tradition, we speak of the behavioral signs that indicate deep spiritual experience, such as when the hairs of the body stand on end and tears flow from the eyes.

Unlike Bede Griffiths, but like Father Thomas Keating (a Trappist monk like Thomas Merton and the architect of a contemporary Christian contemplative tradition known as Centering Prayer), John Main's approach emphasized the rediscovery of contemplative practices within the Christian tradition itself. When we met for a private session in Father John's urban retreat house in Montreal, he gave me a copy of *The Rule of Saint Benedict.* So, in 1994 I was asked to lead the John Main Seminar by Father Laurence Freeman, whom I came to appreciate as a spiritual brother. Father Laurence gave me the difficult assignment of commenting on a series of passages that he had selected from the four Gospels. And subsequently a little book called *The Good Heart: A Buddhist Perspective on the Teachings of Jesus* was published as a record of this meeting.

It became clear in the course of our three-day dialogue, when we were joined by a number of other Christians and Buddhists, including Sister Eileen O'Hea and Ajahn Amaro, that discussion between sincere practitioners of Christianity and Buddhism can be mutually enriching and spiritually sustaining for both parties. Another important contemporary Christian teacher active in promoting contemplative practice is Brother David Steindl Rast who is known simply as Brother David. A contemporary of the late Thomas Merton, Brother David has been most active in the inter-religious dialogue and experience and I have met with him on a number of occasions.

Side by side with complex theological approaches, such as in Roman Catholicism and Orthodoxy, Christianity embraces a faith based on a direct relationship between the individual and God. This relationship is particularly pronounced in the various Protestant denominations, with their emphasis on faith as a movement of the heart rooted in a total trust in God's love. As Martin Luther, on whose teachings the Protestant faith is based, stated, "Everyone must do his own believing as he will have to do his own dying." Here the powerful drive is an intimate and a personal relationship with

God, mediated by one's conscience and also by the redeeming story of Jesus' life and passion. Given this individual relationship with the Creator, scripture as the living word of God becomes the key reference point in implementing God's will, as revealed to one's own conscience, in the world.

The Way of Contemplation

Merton, Griffiths, Main, Keating, and David all represent contemporary attempts on the part of sincere Christians to revive the rich tradition of contemplative practice in Christianity. I have heard of the continuous lineage of Christian meditative practice in the Orthodox tradition, as well as in various Catholic orders such as the Carmelites. I was told that there exists a beautiful Orthodox practice, connected with a commentarial text known as the *Philocalia*, that stresses the injunction of Saint Paul in his First Epistle to the Thessalonians, when he says "pray continually." This prayer became the inspiration for a kind of mantra practice in Orthodoxy consisting of a constant, uninterrupted calling upon the divine name of Jesus with the lips, in the spirit, in the heart, while forming a mental picture of His constant presence and imploring His grace during every occupation, at all times, in all places, even during sleep. The appeal is conducted in these terms: "Lord Jesus Christ, have mercy upon me." Apparently this ancient tradition survived in Russian Orthodoxy at least until the ascendancy of communism. The combination of visualization and incantation, and the making of the incantation into a silent prayer that may be aligned with the heartbeat, evokes a range of possible parallels with ancient Indian meditations.

One issue here is the constant vigilance of the mind at prayer, which Evagrius of Pontus (whom Merton characterized as one of the greatest Christian mystical theologians) described as "a continuous state of intellectual contemplation." This has clear resemblances to the call for continuous mindfulness in Indian traditions, including Buddhism, and the union of tranquillity with insight, which is the key instrument for meditative development. Prayer for eastern Christian mystics like Gregory of Nyssa or Evagrius appears to be the purification of the mind from all passionate thought and all intermediaries (including even the vision of Jesus himself) until there is simply a direct intuition of the Holy Trinity. The path is seen in this context as the renunciation of things, followed by the struggle to be pure of passions and the purification of ignorance, as well as all darkness and dereliction. The imagery shared by many of the more contemplative Christian writers of a journey through darkness and an ascent to light is beautiful. Needless to say, this metaphor of a journey from darkness to light resonates with the Buddhist vision of the path from the darkness of ignorance to the light of wisdom, understanding, and ultimate reality.

Listening to Father Eugene McCaffrey and Father Paul Murray, both of whom participated in a discussion with me, hosted by the noted scholar Father Richard Finn, on contemplative prayer in Christianity and Buddhism (held at Blackfriars, the Dominican college in the University of Oxford, in 2008), I was impressed by striking similarities not only of experience but even of the language used to evoke it. I listened to Father Eugene's presentation almost in the manner of following a guided meditation, and I felt a deep connection between Saint John of the Cross's (1542–1591) vision of the journey of the soul in its search for the Divine within and the Buddhist meditation on the dissolution of self. In both of these cases, the individual is led powerfully through stages of increasing loss of self identity to an utterly radical vision of existence beyond the bounds of individual selfhood. Even John of the Cross's description of the terror, the sense of loss, in what he calls "the dark night" echoes the phenomenological descriptions of the no-self experience in the Buddhist contemplative tradition, where the meditator who dissolves a sense of the solidity of self comes to confront what is called "terror in the face of emptiness." Saint John of the Cross was one of Spain's greatest poets and theologians. In describing the profound experience of the ecstasy of high contemplation, he says how this state transcends the bounds of language and thought:

> I entered into unknowing,
> yet when I saw myself there,
> without knowing where I was,
> I understood great things;
> I will not say what I felt
> for I remained in unknowing
> transcending all knowledge.
>
> That perfect knowledge
> was of peace and holiness
> held at no remove
> .in profound solitude;
> it was something so secret
> that I was left stammering,
> transcending all knowledge.
>
> I was so overwhelmed,
> so absorbed and withdrawn,
> that my senses were left

> deprived of all their sensing,
> and my spirit was given
> an understanding while not understanding,
> transcending all knowledge.
>
> ("THE DARK NIGHT," COLLECTED WORKS OF
> ST. JOHN OF THE CROSS)

One aspect of the Christian vision of God—and especially of his having a Son who was human—is the possibility of identifying with Jesus and using the model of Jesus as a means for spiritual transcendence. Although Buddhists do not regard any of the Buddhas as anything other than men or women who attained enlightenment, it remains possible to identify with the Buddha as an object of contemplation—especially in the intense visualizations of the Buddhist Vajrayana tradition—in ways perhaps quite similar to Christianity. Likewise, the worship of Jesus as a supreme being, especially in the form of prayers of penitence or petition, has parallels with some forms of devotional Buddhism, such as the prayer for salvation to Amitabha Buddha in the Pure Land tradition.

Perhaps it is fair to say that among all the great religions of the world, it is Christianity, particularly Roman Catholicism, with which I have had closest contact outside of Buddhism. This might have had something to do with the fact that Thomas Merton represented Christianity so well at our seminal meetings in the early years of my exile in northern India. I also credit the subsequent friendships I developed with Catholic teachers like John Main, Bede Griffiths, Thomas Keating, and Laurence Freeman, all involving active interreligious dialogue. Given Christianity's unmistakable message of love and compassion, the New Testament's focus on compassion as the defining truth of God—God as infinite love, a Divinity who cares for the suffering of the world—resonates powerfully with the Buddhist emphasis on the centrality of compassion as the highest spiritual and ethical value. Once, at a public talk in Sydney, Australia, I was introduced by the Reverend Bill Crews, of the Ashfield Parish Mission, whom I have over the years come to know as a good friend. In describing my life and work, the pastor said that he considered me a good Christian! Clearly, he knows that I am a Buddhist, and a staunch one at that. However, inasmuch as possible I try to bring to my life and work the ideal of compassion, which is a value that I most cherish—thus, my pastor friend is right in characterizing me as a "good Christian."

Let me conclude this chapter on my engagement with Christianity with words that I once wrote as part of an introduction to Martin Kitchen's *Word of Promise* a publication on The Epistle of James from the New Testament.

> When we read the Bible today, it reminds us that not only are many of our fundamental spiritual values universal, they are also perennial. So long as human beings' fundamental nature, aspiring for happiness and wishing to overcome suffering, remains unchanged, these basic values will remain relevant to us, both as individual human beings and as a society.

If we ask what these values are in essence, they come down to the compassion embodied in Jesus that is beautifully captured in the scriptural commandment "Thou shalt love thy neighbor as thyself."

For a Buddhist, this is the essence of the practice of love and compassion.

5

ISLAM:

SUBMISSION

TO GOD

Absolute Submission to God

One thing immediately recognizable in Islam is the sheer dedication
to the observance of regular daily prayer, called *Salah* in Arabic and
Namaz in Turkish and Persian, which is undertaken five times a day.
From the early morning, the call for prayers resounds from the towering minarets wherever there is a substantial community of Muslims. In fact, right next to Buddhism's most holy place, the *stupa* at
Bodh Gaya that commemorates the site of the Buddha's enlightenment more than 2,500 years ago, there is a mosque that issues the
typical Islamic call for prayer, *"Allahu Akbar,"* literally "God is Great,"
at dawn every morning, which you can hear as you walk around the
stupa. These calls for prayer are sung in a beautiful cascading chant
that conjures up the image of a voice traveling across the Middle
Eastern desert and helps connect the faithful with the awareness of

the Divine. When I had the opportunity to visit an Islamic country in the Middle East—Jordan in 2005—and heard the calls for prayer from the mosques in Amman, it was most impressive. The thought that right then, at that very moment, millions of people were collectively taking a pause, however brief, from their lives, to turn their thoughts toward God, moved me deeply.

The great feature of Islam that first struck me powerfully, and continues to do so, is the single-pointedness with which Muslims relate to God. There is an unconditional embracing of God's absolute transcendence, be it in terms of language and thought or of form. In the Islamic tradition, this transcendence goes side by side with a stress on the immanence of God, beautifully captured in one quotation from the Qur'an: God is "closer to [man] than his jugular vein" (50:16). Islam proclaims an uncompromising espousal of the infinite and the atemporal nature of God and is effectively a duty to relate to God directly at this level. Representation of God in any form is strongly discouraged, for this may slide into idolatry; hence, the absence of images in Islamic places of worship. This single-pointedness and the directness of the faithful's approach to God are beautifully conveyed in the very opening passages of the Holy Qur'an:

> In the name of God, the Compassionate and the Merciful.
> Praise be to God, Lord of the Universe,
> The Compassionate, the Merciful,
> Sovereign of the Day of Judgment!
> You alone we worship, and to You alone we turn for help.
> Guide us to the straight path,
> The path of those whom You have favored . . .
>
> (SURAH I)

The focus on God is so central that the very name *Islam* has the connotation of total submission to God. The word, I am told, is derived from the Arabic for "to accept," "to surrender," or "to submit." As a religion, what is central in Islam is a submission of the individual to the will of God. Since God is characterized as the Compassionate and the Merciful, in my understanding, the faithful are actually offering an absolute submission to the ideal of universal compassion. By way of such submission, God's compassion can flow through the actions of the faithful. In my own Buddhist tradition, there is a similar practice in which one offers one's entire being as a servant to the embodiment of compassion.

To an outsider, especially a secular person, Islam's uncompromising submission to God may seem difficult to comprehend, and this can lead to crude misconstruings of this submission as a form of religious fundamentalism. But for the devout Muslim God is absolute and beyond form; and our duty, as finite creatures bound in the limitations of time and space, is to bow down in the presence of this profound mystery.

My engagement with Islam is unfortunately less deep than that with the other world religions. Until very recently I have not been able to visit any Muslim countries in the Middle East, nor to establish deep friendships with Muslim religious leaders from that part of the world. My best contacts have been with Muslims in India or the West. In India—a country with one of the largest Islamic populations in the world—I have had longstanding personal friendships with several devout Ladakhi Muslims, including an imam from a remote part of Ladakh in northern India. Since a large percentage of the people of Ladakh are traditionally Tibetan Buddhists, and also given that there is a Tibetan refugee settlement and a Tibetan children's village near Leh, the principal city in Ladakh, I visit the region quite often. I have a modest retreat house outside Leh where I like to undertake meditation retreats whenever I can take some time off. During these visits I regularly use the opportunity to meet with my Muslim friends for a cup of tea or a meal. Over time, through discussions as well as my visits to the local mosques, the Muslim congregations of these imams and their Buddhist neighbors have become good friends. In our discussions, one Shia Ladakhi told me that, according to his understanding of the Qur'an, any person who causes bloodshed to his fellow human beings is not a true Muslim. Another stated that a true Muslim must love God's creatures as much as he loves Allah. This is beautiful. Of course, the language used in Islam to articulate its vision of universal compassion is different from that of Buddhism, but the concept and its spiritual effect on an individual's ethical life are not different here from the fundamental Buddhist tenet of compassion for all sentient beings.

The Prophet and the Faithful

Central to the faith of all Muslims is the belief that Muhammad is God's last prophet on earth and that the Qur'an constitutes God's final revelation of truth. The story of how Muhammad came to be chosen as God's messenger remains a source of deep inspiration for all devout Muslims. According to tradition, Muhammad was born in 570 CE into a leading tribe from Mecca. He suffered much personal tragedy during his childhood; the turning point came when he married a widow named Khadija, who was fifteen years his senior and remained the Prophet's trusted friend all her life. Around 610 CE, Muhammad received his commission from God as God's Prophet. This momentous event occurred on the outskirts of Mecca at Mount Hira. Thus began God's revelation through the Angel Gabriel, which came to be recorded in the text of the Qur'an. For Muslims, the Qur'an represents the true word of God. It is unlike any other text— it is not a human creation, nor is it adulterated with the limitations of any human intention or thought. Literally, the Qur'an is God's greatest miracle, and therefore not only is its content perfect but even the language in which it is uttered is perfect. This explains why, for a devout Muslim, the only acceptable version of the Qur'an is the original Arabic—no translation is fully legitimate. In addition to the Qur'an, Islam accepts the authority of another set of scriptures known as the Hadith, literally the sayings of the Prophet, which were later compiled to form a collection. These two texts together provide guidance for the life of the faithful in the Islamic tradition.

Historically, the followers of the Prophet evolved into two main traditions: Sunni, the "traditionalists", and Shia, meaning the partisans of Ali, the Prophet's son-in-law. The Sunnis are in the majority in most Islamic countries, except for Iran and Iraq. Doctrinally, there are no major differences between these two Islamic traditions— their absolute devotion to Allah, their deep faith that the Qur'an represents God's final revelation, and the belief that Muhammad is God's true Prophet are shared by both. When it comes to the interpretation of the subtle nuances of Sharia law, there are many and diverse legal schools of interpretation in both traditions. The key difference has to do with the historical dispute over the question of the Prophet's succession, with the Shi'ites believing that Muhammad's son-in-law Ali should have been the successor following the

Prophet's death. I have often asked my various Muslim friends, such as Dalil Boubakeur, the rector of the Mosque de Paris, about the difference between Sunni and Shia Islam, and have come to recognize that the division has no doctrinal basis at all. I first met Boubakeur in France in 1993, when he and I were part of an interfaith gathering that included a pilgrimage to Lourdes. Subsequently he invited me to visit his mosque.

Five Pillars of Islam

When it comes to everyday practice, there are the five duties incumbent on every Muslim. These are Shahadah (profession of faith), Salah (ritual prayer), Zakat (almsgiving), Sawm (fasting), and Hajj (pilgrimage to Mecca). These five duties succinctly embody the spirit, goal, and deeds of a devout Muslim who dedicates his or her life to pursuing the ideal of submission to the will of Allah. These five pillars, although they may be enshrined in doctrine, are not themselves doctrinal, but they represent practices of the faithful. As such, I see many parallels with sincere religious practice of other traditions, including my own Buddhist faith.

1. *Shahadah* (profession of faith). Every Muslim must say, "There is no god but Allah, and Muhammad is His messenger." As the most important pillar, this testament is a foundation for all other beliefs and practices. Ideally, these are the first words a newborn will hear, and they will be recited when he or she dies. Muslims must repeat the Shahadah in prayer. The parallel in Buddhism would be taking refuge in the Three Jewels—the

Buddha, the Dharma (his teaching), and the Sangha (the spiritual community). In Buddhism, too, seeking refuge in the Three Jewels is an affirmation of one's faith.

2. *Salah* (ritual prayer). Prayer is performed facing the Kaaba in Mecca and is intended to focus the mind on Allah; it is seen as a personal communication with Allah, expressing gratitude and worship. According to the Qur'an, the benefit of prayer "restrains [one] from shameful and evil deeds." (Qur'an 29:40). Salah is to be performed five times a day, and it is compulsory, but some flexibility in the specifics is allowed depending on circumstances. In Buddhist tradition, the devout recite passages of scriptures that evoke the sense of impermanence and the transient nature of existence so as to turn the mind away from inclining toward unwholesome deeds. The key mental faculties to be applied in this context are the sense of shame and a regard for others.

3. *Zakat* (almsgiving). Enjoined on the believer in the Qur'an, Zakat, or almsgiving, is the practice of charitable giving and is obligatory for all who are able to do it. It is considered to be a personal responsibility for Muslims to ease economic hardship for others and to eliminate inequality. Zakat consists of spending a fixed portion of one's wealth for the benefit of the poor or needy, including slaves, debtors, and travelers. I am told that, in the past, some Muslim communities maintained the custom of farmers leaving a small corner of their fields unharvested, which were for the poor to help themselves. (In fact, I believe there is a similar commandment in the Judeo-Christian scriptures.) This is wonderful, for it suggests that while giving charity to the poor, the devout must also ensure that the dignity of the poor is respected. The spiritual meaning of this practice is the generosity of the heart toward those poorer than oneself. I

find it hugely heartening that Islam places generosity at the very center of its religious practice. In Buddhism, *dana* (or generosity) is the first of the perfections that a sincere practitioner aims to cultivate; it is the ground on which a firm commitment to compassion must be based. In the Tibetan tradition, there is the expression "Offerings to the Three Jewels, and almsgiving to the poor and needy." What makes the Islamic practice of Zakat so special is the formalization of this charity as an institution, thus narrowing the gap between ideal and actuality.

4. *Sawm* (fasting). There are three types of fasting recognized by the Qur'an: ritual fasting, fasting as compensation or repentance, and ascetic fasting. While fasting after midday is one of the precepts of a monk in the Buddhist tradition, it is impressive that Islam has extended this restraint of the senses to all practitioners, especially during the holy month of Ramadan.

5. *Hajj* (pilgrimage). The Hajj is a pilgrimage to the holy city of Mecca during the Islamic month of Dhu al-Hijjah. All ablebodied Muslims are obliged to make the pilgrimage to Mecca at least once in their lifetime, if they can afford it. When the pilgrim is around ten kilometers from Mecca, he must dress in Ihram clothing, which consists of two white sheets. The main rituals of the Hajj include walking seven times around the Kaaba, touching the Black Stone, traveling seven times between Mount Safa and Mount Marwah, and symbolically "Stoning the Devil" in Mina. The Hajj also includes a visit to Medina, the second holiest city of Islam. The pilgrim, or the *haji,* is honored on the return to his or her home community. Islamic teachers say that the Hajj should be an expression of devotion to Allah, not a means to gain social standing. One of the things that is remarkable about the Hajj is that, during the actual pilgrimage,

there are no distinctions of class, wealth, or race among pilgrims: all are equal in the presence of God. Pilgrimage in Buddhism is much less formal and not at all institutionalized. However, visiting the key sites associated with the Buddha's life and the sacred places connected with great sages or meditators is recognized as an important part of religious life.

Islam and Buddhism

The history of relations between Islam and Buddhism, at least on the Indian subcontinent, has been fraught with tragedy. It was at the hands of central Asian Muslim invaders that some of Buddhism's greatest monastic institutions came to be destroyed. Although my own homeland is known, and correctly so, as a devout Buddhist land, few know that it has been home to a Muslim community for nearly four hundred years. According to some historians, Kashmiri Muslims settled in central Tibet as early as the twelfth century. It was during the rule of the Fifth Dalai Lama, one of my most illustrious predecessors in the line of the Dalai Lamas, that a full-fledged community of Muslims came to be established in Tibet. It turns out that there was a widespread famine in Kashmir in the mid-seventeenth century, and a number of Kashimiri Muslims sought refuge in Lhasa. The Fifth Dalai Lama granted the Muslims special privileges; he gave them land for a mosque and a cemetery, permitted them to elect a five-member committee to supervise their internal affairs, allowed them to settle their disputes independently, and exempted them from taxes.

When I grew up as a child in Lhasa I had personal contacts with local Tibetan Muslims. One of them was an expert clock repairer. I had a pocket watch then, which I believe had belonged to my immediate predecessor, the Thirteenth Dalai Lama. When this watch stopped working I called this repairer to mend it. After he had done so, the old Muslim gave me, the young Dalai Lama, some sound advice. He said: "The person who is carrying a watch in his pocket should be careful and behave as if he is carrying an egg." To a restless boy this was a sobering thought! When I fled into exile in 1959, a number of Muslims came after me—being no less loyal to the cause of a free Tibet than other Tibetans. Several have served in the Tibetan government in exile for a long period, and continue to do so.

During my first visit to Jordan in 2005 I had a series of private conversations with a noted scholar in the Sufi, or mystical, tradition of Islam. He was deeply interested in exploring how Islamic theologians might understand aspects of Buddhism that demonstrate it as a great spiritual tradition. I acknowledged that the absence of a transcendent God and an eternal soul mark Buddhism apart from a religion like Islam, but I pointed out that, unlike secular philosophies, in Buddhism there is a notion of salvation (or enlightenment) that is defined as a sentient being's ultimate end. There is also an acceptance of higher beings, such as the buddhas and bodhisattvas, whom the faithful may offer prayers to and seek blessings from. Finally, there is the notion of ultimate truth, which the religious seeker can come to know and even to embody. An essential practice in all Buddhist traditions is to seek refuge in the Three Jewels—the Buddha, the Dharma, and the Sangha. One might understand the Dharma as the truth, the Buddha as its perfect embodiment, and the Sangha as the spiritual community that walks in the path of truth. Especially in the Sanskrit tradition of Buddhism, the concept of the threefold embodiment of Buddhahood *(trikaya)* attempts to explain the relationship between the finite and the infinite, between the temporal and the atemporal, between the ultimate and the relative.

One notable Muslim teacher whom I have engaged in a rich dialogue is Dr. Tirmiziou Diallo, a hereditary Sufi religious leader from Guinea, West Africa, who had spent many years in exile in Germany after a communist takeover in his native land. In fact, he came to see me at my residence in Dharamsala, northern India. We discussed the Sufi meditative practices of Diallo's own tradition, and especially the West African lineages that espouse the practice of compassion. Another Sufi master who came to see me was Piern Felad, with whom earlier I had had conversations in France and the United States. We discussed the similarities between the Sufi mystical tradition and certain meditative practices in Mahayana Buddhism.

Compassion in Islam

To an outsider like myself one wonderful feature of Islam is its enshrinement of compassion as a spiritual and ethical principle. The Qur'an repeatedly stresses compassion in the opening lines (which appear before each of its *suras,* or chapters) invoking the name of God, "the Compassionate and the Merciful." There are numerous references to the compassion of God in addition to the *sura* openings—for instance, "God's grace and mercy, His compassion and forgiveness" (24:20) or "God is Compassionate toward His servants" (3:30). The Qur'an might be said to teach compassion through the path of submission to God, and hence through the individual's becoming an instrument of the working of God's own mercy and compassion.

Once we have a recognition of compassion as a key spiritual value in Islam, we will not be swayed by those who wish to portray Islam as inherently violent. These include both people from inside the tradition and those on the outside who present Islam as a militant religion. To appreciate the place of compassion in Islam is, I believe, crucially important in the wake of the catastrophe of September 11. On the first anniversary of this tragedy, I spoke at the National Cathedral in Washington, D.C., and I took the opportunity to warn the Americans not to be swayed by the popular media's increasing portrayal of Islam as a militant faith. I argued that just because a handful of Muslims perpetrated the horrific crime of 9/11, this did not mean that all Muslims were terrorists. A handful of mischievous Muslims cannot represent the tradition as a whole, and blaming the entire faith because of the behavior of a few is totally unfair. I reminded the gathering that unruly people can be found in practically all religions—Buddhism, Christianity, Judaism, and Hinduism included.

Given my personal commitment to inter-religious understanding and harmony, ever since that memorial service in Washington, D.C., I have made special efforts to reach out to the Islamic world, with the aim that its members do not feel alienated from the world's other major religious traditions and also to persuade others of the essentially nonviolent nature of Islam. In India, the Muslim community is particularly keen on engaging in inter-religious activities and is strongly welcoming of the practitioners of other faiths. When I went recently to pray in a white cap in the Jama Masjid in Delhi, I was accorded a warm welcome and was graciously received. Likewise, when I was invited to speak at an inter-religious conference on the theme of world religions after 9/11, at the Islamic university of Jamai Ismail in New Delhi, I felt that there was a genuine eagerness for contact and discussion. On the international level, there are a number of figures who have their feet in both the Muslim and the Western worlds, such as Seyyed Hossein Nasr, a great expert on Sufism and a professor in America, who can play an important role. I have always been impressed by his brilliant articulation and his solid grasp of both East and West. Similarly, once at Emory University, in Atlanta, at a conference on science and religion, the noted Islamic legal scholar Abdullahi Ahmed An-Na'im, who was originally from Sudan, gave a clear presentation of the essence of Islam and responded powerfully to popular and common misconceptions of the tradition.

As part of my own effort to bring the Islamic world and other religions closer together, in San Francisco in 2006 I participated in a gathering of Muslim religious leaders and scholars from many Middle Eastern and African nations. It was hosted by my friend Imam Mehdi Khorasani, the imam of Marin County, California, and attended also by Sayyid Syeed, national director for the office of Interfaith and Community Alliances of the Islamic Society of North America (ISNA). There were also representatives of other faith traditions, including my old friend the noted religious scholar Huston Smith. The gathering discussed how to mitigate religious intolerance by promoting understanding and compassion among peoples of all faiths. I stressed how I see compassion to be at the heart of the teaching of Islam, and how the time has come for the followers of the world's great religions to come together to work toward the creation of a more compassionate and peaceful world.

Believing in the power of personal contact, I have recently been to the great festival at the Ajmer Sharif shrine in Rajasthan, one of the holiest Sufi sites in India. Muslim pilgrims from all parts of the Indian subcontinent take part in a night-long session of prayer on the occasion of Urs, the anniversary of the death of the Sufi saint Khwaja Mu'inuddin Chishti, which begins around 10 PM and ends about 6 AM the next morning. Over one hundred thousand pilgrims shared their devotions in what was to me a most moving spiritual experience. This annual gathering is one of the largest congregations of Muslims at any one place after Mecca, with pilgrims from all over the Islamic world. I first met the chief imam of Ajmer, S. M. Dewan Sayyid Zainul Abedin Ali Khan, at the consecration of the memorial to the late Jain teacher Acharya Sushil Kumar in Delhi. We felt an immediate rapport and he extended a kind invitation to me to attend the pilgrimage.

Later I felt touched to be invited to participate at a conference on terrorism in New Delhi in 2008, which was organized by the Jama Masjid United Forum and attended by Muslims also from Indonesia, Afghanistan, Pakistan, and Jordan. There, I stressed how important it is for the leaders of the world's faith traditions to declare categorically that violence in the name of one's own religion can never be condoned. It is critical, moreover, for religious leaders constantly to stress the centrality of compassion as a foundational principle in every faith tradition.

I am aware that there is a view, both within and outside Islam, that the concept of jihad defines Islam as a more militant faith than others. This view requires an entirely literal interpretation of verses like: "The true believers fight for the cause of God, but the infidels fight for the devil. Fight then against the friends of Satan" (Qur'an 4:76). Of course, such a literal reading is possible. But I have been told by expert Islamic thinkers that there are certainly other interpretations that take jihad—that is, the concept of holy war—to be an internal spiritual struggle. The literal reading, it seems to me, is incompatible with the Qur'an's repeated invocation of Allah as merciful and compassionate.

Contemplative Practice

One of the most uplifting spiritual teachers in the Islamic tradition, who also happened to be an extraordinary poet and to whose writings I have been exposed, is Jelaluddin Rumi (1207–1273), who was known as Mevlana, an Afghan native who wrote in Persian and lived most of his life in Konya, Turkey. As with the writings of John of the Cross in the Christian tradition, Rumi's ecstatic poems are similar in tone, in spiritual depth, and in immediacy of experience to *nyamgur,* the experiential songs of religious poets in my own Tibetan tradition. For example, the reciprocity of love in Rumi becomes a model for the relationship of spiritual master and pupil, as in the Guru-disciple model of Tibetan Buddhism.

In particular, Rumi wrote a book of poems in honor of his friend and teacher Shams of Tabriz. This reminds me of the yearning of the meditator for his absent master in many examples of Tibetan experiential songs. For instance, I think of this beautiful poem by Milarepa, writing in the eleventh century CE about his master, Marpa:

> To see my father guru's face and hear his voice
> Transforms this beggar's grief into a mystic's revelation.
> Recalling my teacher's exemplary life,
> Reverence dawns deep in my heart.
>
> (SONGS OF SPIRITUAL EXPERIENCE, THUPTEN JINPA AND
> JAŚ ELSNER, SHAMBHALA, 2000)

This kind of spiritual love, and the intense feeling of absence in the separation of spiritual friends, is represented by Rumi, whose poems are often recited at interfaith services, as being the source of his poetic voice and part of his spiritual inspiration:

Love for you took away my rosary, and gave (me) verses and songs . . .
At Love's hand, I became a singer of odes, hand-clapping . . .

(Divān 940, trans. Arberry)

Historically speaking, some of the most open and pluralist mo-
ments in world culture have taken place under Islamic rule.
Whether one thinks of Spain in the Middle Ages, or the Caliphate of
Baghdad, or Akbar's India, literary culture and scientific learning
flourished along with a notable tolerance of religious multiplicity.
Not only was it through Arabic sources that the West came to redis-
cover its Greek philosophical heritage, but these same sources im-
mensely enriched the understanding of mathematics and astronomy
in Indian and Tibetan Buddhism. The perception of Islam as narrow,
intolerant, and even open to terrorism is a false one and a very
unfortunate consequence of 9/11. To take the insane acts of a misguided handful as representative of anything but their own deprav-
ity is to make a generalization that simply has no basis. In the
religious community worldwide we must work unceasingly to reverse this wrong image, and in Islam itself leaders must make clear
to Muslims that the extremist interpretation of their faith is not only
damaging to the tradition but in fact does no justice to the richness
and beauty of what Islam stands for.

6

JUDAISM:

FAITH

OF THE EXILE

Faith and Exile

For the Tibetan people—those under Chinese occupation inside Tibet and the exiles who have fled the land of their ancestors—the image of Judaism as a religion that has helped a people to survive in exile for so long is deeply inspiring. When I first came into contact with Jewish leaders, I used to ask them, "Tell me your secret!" For Judaism has managed to adapt its religious practices to the ways of exile over many centuries and to preserve the key features of its tradition, the kernel of its path, in so many foreign lands and amid foreign customs, even in hostile environments.

Of course, if this were merely a matter of preserving outer forms and defunct rituals, Judaism would have perished swiftly. So the question is less about preserving a specific cultural tradition rooted in a particular homeland and its customs than about finding the essence of one's spiritual tradition and being willing to adapt the forms of one's practice to new situations while fostering, cherishing, and developing what is essential. As a religion it has been subject to remarkable change—impermanence—in response to radically changing conditions of exile and diaspora, especially after the destruction of the Second Temple in Jerusalem in the first century CE. Jews have been the victims of great suffering in these circumstances—and not least in the twentieth century, with their horrific treatment at the hands of the Nazis. During my first visit to Europe in 1973, I had a memorable meeting with a Jewish rabbi in Holland. In discussing the tragedy of the Holocaust, he gave such an intense, moving account of the experience that we were both in tears.

Constantly, over many centuries, the Jewish people have found radical renewal on many levels—not just the political creation of the state of Israel but also numerous reformulations of the nature of Orthodoxy, of different kinds of reform suitable to varying conditions and circumstances, and perhaps above all of spiritual practice in the hands of great Rabbis and masters, such as those who helped to create the Mishnah and reformulate diasporic Judaism after the fall of the Second Temple. To a Tibetan spiritual practitioner, the richness of the mystical element in Judaism is greatly intriguing. While always oriented toward keeping alive what is most spiritual and characteristic in the tradition, the forms of activity forged by these different masters in very different situations exemplify a truly humbling nonattachment to the cruder forms of identity, holding on to which might have prevented the survival of Judaism, or at least what is most valuable in it.

When I first visited Israel in 1994 I met with one of the two chief rabbis of Judaism in Jerusalem. During this meeting, I asked the rabbi what it is that unites Jews the world over—what the kernel of the doctrine is that unites all Jews. His response took me by surprise: "When it comes to doctrine, there is hardly any uniformity. What unites all faithful Jews are the rituals. Come Friday, all Jewish homes, from Siberia to Ethiopia, hold Sabbath in the same manner. We have been doing this for thousands of years, since the destruction of the Temple in Jerusalem." Now, Tibetan Buddhism has a great many rituals of its own, but personally I have never been a great believer in the efficacy of ritual in its own right. So the chief rabbi's answer really came as a surprise. But, as I have thought about it since, what ritual means in the context of exile and diaspora is a particular form of continuity and connection that allows great pluralism of views and beliefs, while at the same time links people through a shared set of practices and a language, biblical Hebrew, to a powerful lineage of memory and tradition. There may be something here for Tibetan Buddhists to learn if it turns out that we have to survive in exile for a long period—I hope not as long as the Jews have had to do.

It was during this visit to Israel that I had a chance to learn more about the long history of the Jewish people. One memorable event was a celebration dedicated to environmental awareness that took place on top of a hill near the resort town of Elat, a vantage point from which one could see three countries—Israel, Jordan, and Egypt. After the meeting, I had the opportunity to visit Masada, a site associated with the important historical event of when the Jewish people rose up to resist their Roman conquerors.

One aspect of the Jewish tradition that has always impressed me is its strong memory of the past—the sense of a lineage reaching back beyond the Second Temple to great biblical figures like Solomon, David, and Moses. The Passover remembrance, "Next year in

Jerusalem," comes to have a range of symbolic resonances much greater than a simple reference to geography or political empowerment. A historical understanding of the past can never be wholly separated, I have noticed in my Jewish friends, from a symbolic and often mystical sense of its meanings. Rabbi Zalman Schachter, for instance, who has been a key participant in a Jewish-Buddhist dialogue that began in 1989 at a small Tibetan Buddhist monastery in New Jersey and culminated in a week-long discussion at my residence in Dharamsala a year later, has a remarkable ability to shift his conversation to see the potential symbolic and spiritual qualities implicit in even apparently mundane topics. It is as if the various rules and many legalisms of Judaism, its numerous rituals carefully observed, can always offer a glimpse of a more profound— even mystical—religious reality that lies just beyond the scope of the naked eye.

At this first formal Buddhist-Jewish dialogue held in New Jersey, representatives from the Orthodox, Conservative, and Reformed traditions of Judaism in America, including a woman rabbi, Joy Levitt, came together. Right from the start, I felt an immediate rapport with Rabbi Zalman. He is a big, bearded man with a rather booming voice, and he appeared familiar with quite a few Buddhist concepts. The rabbis and the Jewish scholars unfolded a scroll of the Torah and also performed a brief prayer with one of the participants even blowing the traditional ram's horn, or shofar. By then I had already heard of the Jewish mystical tradition known as Kabbalah and was eager to know something about it from the experts. It was refreshing to see how divergent the views of most of these rabbis and scholars were on issues that pertain to their Jewish faith. The love of argumentation and critical inquiry that is part of the Jewish heritage came through quite clearly.

Torah and the Talmud

My first visit to a synagogue took place in India. This was in Cochin, Kerala, in 1965. It was then that I first saw the Torah scroll in its impressive case and observed the way it was affectionately looked after. My friend Rabbi Zalman once said to me that there were 613 commandments (or *mitzvot*) expected of the pious Jew. That is more than double the 253 *vinaya* or rules that must be followed by monks in Tibetan Buddhism, who follow the Mulasarvastivada tradition of monastic regulation! It is interesting that Judaism has a rich and vibrant commentary on these laws, as does Buddhism, and that some *mitzvot* can no longer be followed because they relate to when the Second Temple in Jerusalem was still intact. The centrality of debate and disputation in Rabbinic Judaism, and in particular the ways in which the Talmud contains not clear answers about questions of law and regulation but, rather, a record of the debates and positions occupied on all sides of a given question over many centuries, is particularly close to the spirit of training in the Tibetan monastic universities.

Judaism accepts both a written Torah (the scriptural law given by revelation) and an oral Torah, which consists of Rabbinic teachings compiled in the Talmud. This opens a door to a real pluralism of disputation and argument that has been distilled and systematized over the centuries in the Talmud and in additional texts in which the rabbis have examined scripture to make it yield teachings not apparent in a surface reading or superficial interpretation. Listening to my Jewish friends' explanations of the roles and places of the two laws in the Jewish tradition reminded me of the parallel position of the *sutras* (sacred words of the Buddha) and *shastras* (commentarial texts of the tradition) found in Buddhism.

Some Buddhist scholars have even noted the striking similarity between the forms of argumentation found in the Buddhist monastic discipline texts and those found in Jewish scholastic works. An important aspect of these analyses is their development and application of sophisticated hermeneutic tools. For example, in the scholastic analysis of the monastic disciplinary codes in Buddhism, distinction is drawn between a principle underlying a precept and its application within a given context. In addition, there is the need to take into account the sensitivity to context so that what may be generally prohibited might actually be not just permissible but obligatory in specific circumstances. In fact, the Buddhist monastic texts speak of numerous different permutations pertaining to the monastic rules.

Mystic Judaism and Buddhism

In Jewish mysticism and meditative practice, as I understand it, there are a number of quite striking similarities with Buddhist practices and attitudes. I think of visualizations, for example, of which there is a remarkable ancient Jewish tradition. In the Bible, there are a series of visions of the divine, characterized not only by such "dark" visions of God as that of Moses in the cleft of rock on Mount Sinai, when the prophet is shown "the back" of God but not His face (Exod. 33:18–23), but also by the great vision of Ezekiel:

> I looked, and I saw a windstorm coming out of the
> north—an immense cloud with flashing lightning and
> surrounded by brilliant light. The center of the fire looked

like glowing metal, and in the fire was what looked like four living creatures. In appearance their form was that of a man, but each of them had four faces and four wings. Their legs were straight; their feet were like those of a calf and gleamed like burnished bronze. Under their wings on their four sides they had the hands of a man. All four of them had faces and wings, and their wings touched one another. Each one went straight ahead; they did not turn as they moved. Their faces looked like this: Each of the four had the face of a man, and on the right side each had the face of a lion, and on the left the face of an ox; each also had the face of an eagle. Such were their faces. Their wings were spread out upward; each had two wings, one touching the wing of another creature on either side, and two wings covering its body.

(Exek. 1: 4–28)

Here with great precision and vividness, the prophet sees a series of divine beings, with specific but unusual physical characteristics and colors. These appear in the context of a great heavenly throne from which speaks a voice. Of course, the differences between specific *tantric* mandalas and deity visualizations are numerous, but the general parallels are strong in terms of perceiving a divine world, whose colors and beings appear hyper-intense, whose forms and textures are three-dimensional, but that include the meditator so that the vision is not merely as a film being looked at vicariously but of a full, real experience at a supra-mundane level. And I understand that there are many non- and post-biblical visualization traditions in mystical Judaism.

Again, I am told that there are traditions in Kabbalistic and Hasidic prayer that involve techniques of recitation and naming—many of these secret except to initiates, like the Highest Yoga *tantras* of Vajrayana Buddhism—that may be parallel to Buddhist practices of mantra recitation. I have been struck by the way Jewish religious teaching often includes stories of famous rabbis, from the distant past right up until very recent, which are sometimes bitter-sweet and often very funny. Buddhist teaching, too, involves such stories; I think of the biographies of famous meditators like Marpa the Translator and the yogi Milarepa in the Tibetan tradition or the anecdotes about Chan and Zen Masters in the Mahayana traditions of China and Japan. The angels of Kabbalah, on which I was privileged to receive a fascinating presentation from Rabbi Zalman, remind me of the *dakas* and *dakinis* in Buddhism—the multitudes of divine beings that represent different aspects of the human psyche. And I was most surprised to discover that mystical Judaism accepts the notion of rebirth, including that of men and angels into animal realms, just like Buddhism. Indeed, in one of the greatest books of Kabbalah, the Zohar, or The Book of Splendor or Illumination, which was written down in thirteenth-century Spain, it is said: "As long as a person is unsuccessful in his purpose in this world, the Holy One, blessed be He, uproots him and replants him over and over again" (Zohar 1:186b).

Self and Other

One really striking characteristic is the closeness of Jewish mysticism—despite its basis in a monotheistic tradition founded on the axiom of a creator God—to certain aspects of what in Buddhism is called emptiness, or *shunyata*. For example, I was told that in the Hasidic and mystical traditions God is described as Ein Soph, "that which is without limit," or even as *ayin*, "nothing" or "that which is not." This is because nothing can be postulated of the Deity, while the created world is *yesh*, "that which is" or the finite. The task of ecstatic practice in the tradition is the self-forgetfulness that loses all sense of *yesh* in the practicitioner until the divine *ayin* (or nothingness) can be encountered when the practitioner is himself in a state of *ayin*. On this model, the ultimate aim of Hasidism is *bittul ha-yesh*, "the annihilation of self," as one's being merges with the Divine in the contemplation that everything is God.

In a beautiful saying from a second-century collection known as the *Pirke Avot* (Sayings of the Fathers), the centrality of selflessness is stressed in a model of four-way logic that is remarkably close to Buddhist ways of reasoning:

> There are four types among men. One who says "what is mine is mine and what is thine is thine," is a usual type. "What is mine is thine and what is thine is mine," is an ignorant type of man. "What is thine is thine and what is mine is thine," is a saintly type of person. "What is thine is mine and what is mine is mine" is a wicked type of person.
>
> PIRKE AVOT 5:10

Here, the relation of self and other is seen not in terms of the merging of ego with the limitless nothing of God but, rather, in terms of relations of attachment between one human being and another. Selflessness, or the "saintly" path that accepts the other but also gives up one's own to the other, is effectively the flow of compassion between human beings.

Compassion in Judaic Teachings

Compassion in Judaism rests upon the model of the love of God, which is perhaps the supreme injunction. As is famously said in the Bible, "Love the Lord your God with all your heart and with all your soul and with all your strength" (Deut. 6:5).

I am told that in the Zohar this is interpreted very much in terms of the enactment of compassion, so that the love of God is experienced and demonstrated through compassion to other beings. "One who loves God is crowned with loving kindness and spares neither himself nor his money" (Zohar 3:267a). Besides the command to love God is the famous injunction—emphasized and taught also by Jesus—to love one's neighbor as oneself (Lev. 19:18). I understand that this teaching, and especially the question of who precisely is meant by the term *neighbor,* has been the subject of much discussion in the commentaries. Many authorities argue that the meaning must extend beyond a fellow Jew to any fellow human being, and thus ultimately to all people. As it is said in Leviticus 19:34, "The alien living with you must be treated as one of your native-born. Love him as yourself, for you were aliens in Egypt."

Compassion for others, in other words, cannot be separated from the love of God, and the imitation of God is itself a call to act from the impetus of loving-kindness. As in Buddhism, acts of loving-kindness are seen not only as a protection for their doer but also as a means of awakening the flow of compassion on the divine level. In the Zohar, it is said that if a man does kindness on earth, he awakens loving-kindness in heaven, and the day itself is crowned with loving-kindness through him. Similarly if he performs a deed of mercy, he crowns the day with mercy, and it becomes his protector in the hour of need (Zohar 3:92b). The Buddha also taught loving-kindness (*maitri* in Sanskrit) as a protection—for instance, for the monks in the forest against wild animals and snakes. Most important, for the Buddhists, the idea of loving-kindness as the most powerful protector is portrayed in the Buddha's deep immersion in meditation on loving-kindness when he was being attacked by Mara and his allies on the eve of his final awakening under the Bodhi Tree.

The word *hasid* derives, I am told, from the Hebrew *hasad,* which means "loving-kindness," "mercy," or "love" in biblical usage, implying reciprocity of compassionate relations between man and God and man and man. So, according to a famous sage, Judah Loew, the Maharal of Prague (1525–1609):

> Love of all creatures is also love of God, for whoever loves the One God loves all the works that He has made. When one loves God, it is impossible not to love His creatures. The opposite is also true. If one hates the creatures, it is impossible to love God Who created them.
>
> (NESIVOS OLAM, AHAVAS HARÈI, I)

Inevitably in Judaism, the aims of merging with God and the imitation of God both imply the pursuit of compassion. I understand that in the Talmud and in synagogue services, God is referred to as the "Compassionate One" and as the "Father of Compassion." In that human beings, whom the Bible affirms are uniquely created in God's image (Gen. 1:27), should imitate God, the call is for God's creatures to be compassionate. I am told that this message is repeated in the Talmud, which states that Jews are to be compassionate children of compassionate ancestors, and that many of the daily prayers stress the compassion of God.

In Hebrew, I am told, the word for compassion is derived from the word that means "womb." Hence, the Jewish notion of compassion is deeply intimate, linked with the idea of mother, as is stressed in a wonderful verse from the visionary prophet Isaiah: "Can a mother forget the baby at her breast and have no compassion on the child she has borne?" (Isa. 49:15).

Compassion is like a mother's love for all the children of her womb—an idea that appears in Buddhist accounts of compassion, too, where loving-kindness is compared with the love of a mother for her child. The Talmudic rabbis, I gather, considered compassion to be one of the three key distinguishing marks of a Jew. I understand that the emphasis on compassion extends beyond human beings to a sense of love for all beings. Judaism also stresses compassion for animals, with many laws in the Torah that insist on kindness to animals—for example, in the injunction to pious Jews to feed their domestic animals before they themselves sit down to eat.

It is interesting that in some of the most intense mystical visions of the Bible, God's compassion is stressed as well. When Moses stands before God in the cleft of rock: "And the Lord said, 'I will cause all my goodness to pass in front of you, and I will proclaim my name, the Lord, in your presence. I will have mercy on whom I will have mercy, and I will have compassion on whom I will have compassion' " (Exod. 33:19).

Likewise, compassion is stressed in some of the more famous stories in the Bible. For example, when Solomon demonstrates his wisdom, he is confronted by two women who bring a living and a dead child before him. Each claims the living baby is her own. Of course, one is lying. Solomon calls for a swordsman to cut the living child in half and give a half to each. At this point, the woman whose son was alive was filled with compassion for her son and said to the king, "Please, my lord, give her the living baby! Don't kill him!" But the other said, "Neither I nor you shall have him. Cut him in two!"

(1 Kings 3:26). The wisdom of Solomon is more than a ruse to elicit which of the women is really the mother; it also calls forth compassion in the mother, and it uses compassion as the route to truth.

One of the first things that I had heard about the Jews was the idea that they are a chosen people. Initially, I thought this must be analogous to the traditional idea of the Tibetan people being specially chosen by Avalokiteshvara, the Buddha of Compassion, who took a pledge to look after the people of the Land of Snows. However, when my friend Huston Smith, who first visited me in Dharamsala in the late 1960s, explained in greater depth the meaning of this Jewish notion of being chosen, I was deeply impressed. Smith said that during the Jewish exile in Babylon, a profound interpretation of Jewish suffering was developed, which appears in the Bible in the latter part of the Book of Isaiah. According to this account, being chosen by God means carrying the weight of human suffering and that through the suffering of the Jewish people the redemption of all humanity can be effected. This represents an extraordinarily selfless ideal. Whereas in Christianity the redemption of the world is placed on the shoulders of one man, albeit the Son of God, in Judaism, an entire people takes onto itself this responsibility. To a Buddhist like myself, this notion exemplifies the ideal of a community of selfless bodhisattvas working for the good of all beings.

7

COMPASSION: WHERE THE WORLD'S RELIGIONS COME TOGETHER

One of the special joys I have come to appreciate in my journey down the spiritual paths of other faiths is the wonderful privilege of opening my heart and hearing the voice of other traditions speaking clearly and directly. This place of sharing, rooted in the heart, is connected to the fact that the great religions themselves urge their practitioners to open their hearts and let compassion blossom as the core message for living an ethical life. Together and in friendliness, the devotees of the great faith traditions walk along the same path when it comes to living a good life and fostering the ethics of compassion.

Who would not be moved by sayings like the following from the world's sacred scriptures?

> *Blessed are those who hunger and thirst for righteousness,*
> *for they will be filled.*

Blessed are the merciful, for they will be shown mercy.
Blessed are the pure in heart, for they will see God.
Blessed are the peacemakers, for they will be called sons of God.

(MATT. 5:6–9, FROM THE BEATITUDES)

All creatures are God's children, and those dearest to God are
those who treat His children kindly.

(PROPHET MUHAMMAD, HADITH)

Sentient beings trapped in aging and sickness
And tormented by a hundred pains,
Seeing them assailed by the terrors of birth, death and sorrow,
He directs his conduct for their weal.

Sentient beings crushed by wheels of suffering
Within the circle of birth and death,
Seeing this, he seeks the thunderbolt of wisdom
That smashes to dust these wheels of woe.

(GANDAVUYHA MAHAYANA SUTRA)

Although I have heard the beautiful lines from the Beatitudes often
at interfaith services, when I was asked to comment on them at the
John Main Seminar in London, for the first time I immersed myself
in their wonderful spirituality. All of us would wish to find happiness
by being blessed in this way, by being dear through kindness and by
directing our conduct for the good of others, even to smashing to
dust the wheel of suffering. And it is one of the glories of the major
religions that their supreme message is to call us to show the compassion by which such spiritual feats can be achieved. The great religions have the power to lift our hearts and raise our minds to an

elevated expanse of joy and understanding through their shared teachings on compassion.

It is my fundamental conviction that compassion—the natural capacity of the human heart to feel concern for and connection with another being—constitutes a basic aspect of our nature shared by all human beings, as well as being the foundation of our happiness. In this respect, there is not an iota of difference between a believer and a nonbeliever, nor between people of one race or another. All ethical teachings, whether religious or nonreligious, aim to nurture this innate and precious quality, to develop it and to perfect it.

One can identify three broadly distinct approaches within this process. One is the theistic approach where the concept of God underpins the ethical teachings that foster man's emulation of God's own compassion. A second is the nontheistic religious approach, such as that of Buddhism, that invokes the law of causality and the fundamental equality of all beings in their basic aspirations for happiness as the grounding of ethics. The third belongs to the secular or nonreligious approach, whereby no religious concepts are evoked but, rather, recognition of the primacy of compassion may be underpinned by common sense, shared common experience, and scientific findings that demonstrate our deep dependence on others' kindness.

Although the world's religions may differ fundamentally from one other in their metaphysical views, when it comes to their teachings on the actual practice of ethics, there is great convergence. All the faith traditions emphasize a virtuous way of being, the purification of the mind from negative thoughts and impulses, the doing of good deeds, and living a meaningful life. All contain essential moral codes that are designed to help one avoid unwholesome actions and embrace virtues. For example, all traditions have a set of moral precepts for living a life that restrains one from harmful actions while encouraging the cultivation of virtues, notably love, compassion, forgiveness, tolerance, contentment, charitable giving, and service to others. All advocate interaction with others that is based on compassionate consideration of the other. On the part of the devout religious individual, all encourage a life of simplicity and modesty in one's desires, as well as self-discipline and a high degree of moral integrity. Alongside these admonitions, a religious vision centers on a deep recognition of the limits of a purely materialistic and self-centered view of life. In other words, at the heart of all the world's religions is a vision of human life that transcends the boundaries of an individual's physical existence as an embodied, finite, and temporal being. A meaningful life, in all the faith traditions, is one that is lived with an awareness of a supra-mundane dimension.

Basic Religious Ethics

All the world religions teach, at the level of motivation—which is to say one's state of mind—the cultivation of loving-kindness and compassion, while at the level of everyday action, they teach the ethics of restraining from harmful deeds. So, whether it is in the context of one's heart or one's actions in the world and in relation to our fellow beings, essentially the key teaching really is compassion.

As I see it, there are three broadly identifiable stages in the ethical teachings on compassion in the great religions: (1) the ethics of restraint, which is the basic level and involves refraining from actions harmful to self and others; (2) the ethics of compassion, which develops the seeds of empathy in having some regard for the other into an active generation of love and compassion for all other beings; (3) the attainment of pure altruism, which is selfless service without regard for any return or benefit.

The world's great religions show a striking convergence on the ethics of restraint. This outlines the fundamentals of a basic framework of morality that prevents one from acting on one's immediate negative impulses, such as aversion and greed. For example, in Judaism, the Ten Commandments include prohibitions against: murder, adultery, theft, bearing false witness, covetousness—all of which pertain to the ethics of restraint. Christianity, as well as endorsing the Ten Commandments, speaks of the "seven deadly sins," which are lust, gluttony, greed, sloth, anger, envy, and pride.

Similarly, in addition to the Ten Commandments, Islam speaks of seventy major sins, such as committing murder, adultery, and so on. In Hinduism and Jainism, and in Buddhism, there is the notion of negative karma that soils the individual's soul or mind, opening the person to misguided deeds that lead to continued rebirth within a cycle of unenlightened existence.

In my own tradition of Buddhism, at the level of basic ethics, we speak of refraining from the "ten unwholesome deeds:" the three bodily actions, (killing, stealing, and sexual misconduct), the four verbal actions, (telling lies, engaging in divisive speech, using harsh words, and senseless gossip), and the three mental actions (covetousness, harmful intent, and harboring wrong views). Together, these ten deeds are understood to constitute the family of unwholesome physical, verbal, and mental actions that are, in turn, outer expressions of the "three poisons of the mind"—greed, aversion, and delusion.

If you look carefully, it comes as no surprise to discover that underlying the world religions' moral teachings, especially as they pertain to the ethics of restraint, is an important ethical principle, often referred to as the Golden Rule. In essence, the idea is that a person's behavior toward others should be guided by the way he wishes them to behave toward him. In particular, one should refrain from those actions one wishes others not to commit against oneself. The key consideration here is the logic of reciprocity. The first time I saw this clearly was at an interfaith service in New York a few years ago. In the program leaflet, the organizers included a list of the ways in which this fundamental ethical principle has been formulated in the world's different faith traditions. For instance:

- Hinduism: *"This is the sum of duty; do naught onto others what you would not have them do unto you"* (Mahabharata 5:1517)
- Judaism: *"What is hateful to you, do not do to your fellowman. This is the entire Law; all the rest is commentary"* (Hillel, in the Talmud for the Sabbath 31a)
- Zoroastrianism: *"That nature alone is good which refrains from doing to another whatsoever is not good for itself"* (Dadisten-I-dinik 94:5)
- Buddhism: *"Since others too care for their own selves, those who care for themselves should not hurt others"* (Udanavarga 5:20)
- Jainism: *"A man should wander about treating all creatures as he himself would be treated"* (Sutrakritanga 1.11:33)
- Daoism: *"Regard your neighbor's gain as your gain, and your neighbor's loss as your own loss"* (Tai-shang Kan-ying P'ien)
- Confucianism: *"Do not do to others what you would not like yourself. Then there will be no resentment against you, either in the family or in the state"* (Analects 12:2)

- Christianity: *"So in everything, do to others what you would have them do to you, for this sums up the Law and the Prophets"* (Matt. 7:12)
- Islam: *"No one of you is a believer until he desires for his brother that which he desires for himself"* (Hadith of al-Nawawi 13)

The key consideration underlying the ethics of restraint in all of the world's religions is the avoidance of doing harm to others. In that sense, even at this basic level, the fundamental value that underpins the moral precepts in the faith traditions is really compassion, in that there is a conscious regard for others. If one looks at the various lists of "sins" — by which I mean actions that one ought *not* to do, such as killing, stealing, adultery, lying, and so forth — they all involve varying degrees and kinds of harm against others. Clearly, the ways in which these precepts are grounded or justified in the faith traditions will differ. A theistic tradition may base the validity of these teachings on divine law, while a nontheistic religion may ground it in the law of causality or on a notion of the basic goodness of our fundamental nature. But the fact remains that, when it comes to the actual content of our moral precepts, and more important, the compassionate ideal they are designed to elicit — there is very little difference between the faiths. From a social-historical point of view, it is amazing that so many different religions — which have evolved in such different places, among different cultures and in different contexts, and have developed such strikingly different theologies and concepts — should have converged when it comes to prescribing how to live a good, ethical life.

The Ethics of Compassion

What we find in the teachings of the world religions is a vision of ethics that moves beyond the limited reciprocity of the Golden Rule to an exhortation to universal compassion. On this level, beyond grounding one's ethics in a *self*-referential framework—that is, "*I* do not do to others what I wish them not to do to *me*"—the world's religions situate this ethics within a larger frame that extends beyond the boundaries of self-reference. In the Golden Rule, there is the seed of compassion because the consideration of the other is central, but in the ethics of compassion, one must move beyond to a plane of genuine selflessness, which I see as a matter of fostering the qualities of a good heart. I often think of my mother as my first teacher of compassion. She was simple, uneducated, just a village farmer, but so kind-hearted—and her kindness was unconditional. It is the love with which she nurtured me that is the core of the compassion I can find in myself and feel for others. This very basic level of affection is natural to human beings, even attributable to our biology, and it is this quality that the religions build upon and enhance.

That a vision of selfless compassion is at the heart of the ethical teachings of the world's major religions is borne out by a cursory glance at their scriptures. For example, a friend of mine has drawn my attention to the following Jewish story in the Mishnaic, *Pirke Avot:*

> Rabbi Yohanan ben Zakkai said, "Go forth and see which is the good way that a man should follow." Rabbi Eliezar said, "A good eye"; Rabbi Joshua said, "A good friend"; Rabbi Jose said, "A good neighbor"; Rabbi Simeon said, "One who foresees the fruit of an action"; Rabbi Elazar

said, "A good heart." Thereupon he said to them, "I ap-
prove the words of Elazar, rather than your words, for in
his words yours are included."

(2:13)

Here, what we find is the teaching that qualities such as the eye of
insight, friendship, neighborliness, and foresight about the effects of
one's actions are all included in the quality of the good heart that is
filled with compassion. This phrase, the "good heart," for me summarizes what is best in human nature.

In the ancient Chinese traditions there is the following celebrated saying in the Confucian classic, The Analects: "Confucius
said, 'Shen, there is one thread that runs through my doctrines.'
Tseng Tsu said, 'Yes.' After Confucius had left, the disciples asked
him, 'What did he mean?' Tseng Tsu replied, 'The Way of our master
is none other than conscientiousness and altruism' " (4:15).

Similarly, in Daoism, the Daodejing states:

> Because of compassion, I can be brave
> Because of moderation, I can be generous . . .
> When heaven wants to establish someone,
> It encircles him with compassion.
>
> (CHAP. 67)

In Christianity, there is a very famous saying of Jesus, based on
the Hebrew Bible: "Love the Lord your God with all your heart and
with all your soul and with all your mind." This is the first and greatest commandment. And the second is like it: "Love your neighbor as
yourself." All the Law and the Prophets hang on these two commandments (Matt. 22:37–40). To my understanding, the beauty of this

teaching is the extraordinary simplicity with which Jesus summarizes the essence of the logic of a spiritual ethics. In a theistic tradition, the core of spiritual practice is to love and *imitate* the Creator. That love of God is exemplified in the Second Commandment, "Love your neighbor as yourself." I often think that in the Judeo-Christian exhortation of "Love your neighbor" Jesus is effectively suggesting that the true test of one's love of God is how much one loves one's fellow human beings.

In Buddhism, in the sutra on loving-kindness, the Buddha says:

> As a mother would risk her life
> to protect her child, her only child,
> Even so should one cultivate a limitless heart
> with regard to all beings.
> With good will for the entire cosmos,
> cultivate a limitless heart:
> Above, below, and all around,
> Unobstructed, without enmity or hate.
> Whether standing, walking,
> Sitting, or lying down,
> As long as one is alert,
> One should be resolved on this mindfulness.
>
> (METTA SUTTA, FROM THE SUTTA NIPATA 1:8)

Here, the most natural bond of affection between human beings, the unconditional love of a mother for her child, is taken as a model for the degree of compassion with which a practitioner is encouraged to approach all beings.

In Hinduism, one finds the following in the great epic, the Ramayana, which is so dear to the hearts of the Indian people:

> A superior being does not render evil for evil; this is a maxim one should observe; the ornament of virtuous persons is their conduct. One should never harm the wicked, or the good, or even criminals meriting death. A noble soul will ever exercise compassion, even towards those who enjoy injuring others.
>
> (YUDDHA KANDA: 115)

In the Qur'an, one reads: "We feed you for God's sake only, we seek of you neither recompense nor thanks" (Qur'an 76:8-9). In addition, I have heard the following saying attributed to the Prophet from the collections know as the Hadith: "A man once asked the Prophet what was the best thing in Islam, and the latter replied, 'It is to feed the hungry and give the greeting of peace both to those one knows and to those one does not know' " (Hadith of Bukhari).

In Sikhism, in the Adi Granth, it is written: "One who serves and seeks no recompense finds union with the Lord. Such a servant alone takes the master's guidance, says Nanak, as on him is divine grace" (Sukhmani Sahib 18:M.5).

In Jainism, in the Tattvartha Sutra, one reads: "The observer of vows should cultivate friendliness toward all living being, delight in the distinction and honor of others, compassion for the miserable, lowly creatures, and equanimity toward the vainglorious" (7.6).

What is particularly moving about this last scriptural citation, but also about the Hadith from the Prophet Muhammad, is the explicit emphasis on the universality of the object of one's compassion. In fact, that one must embrace all beings within the folds of one's compassionate concern is not only explicit in all traditions but also essential. Whether one thinks of others as being God's creatures or as "mother sentient beings"—that is, the Buddhist view that in the limitless turning of rebirths all beings have at some point been one's mother—what matters is the direct link of heart to heart within the totality of the sentient world.

In this variety of teachings from the different traditions, as exemplified in the citations above, the religious injunction to compassion is revealed to be more than the Golden Rule, that ethics of reciprocity defined by treating others as you would yourself like to be treated. In the faith traditions, treatment of others as you wish yourself to be treated is only a first step on a path that ultimately aims to move you to where consideration of how yourself is treated no longer plays any role, but becomes simply a medium for compassionate action. How, at its highest level, such a selfless being may become a vessel for the outpouring of compassion is beautifully exemplified in the verses of Nagarjuna, the second-century teacher deeply revered in my Tibetan tradition:

> Like the earth, water, and wind,
> And like medicine and the trees in the forest,
> Offer your own self to others, even for an instant,
> To be used by others as they may wish.
> (PRECIOUS GARLAND 3:58)

The model of turning the other cheek, or of having an overriding compassion for all beings, however they treat you, is about the elimination of self-centeredness and the cultivation of qualities that—in a theistic tradition—bring the practitioner ever closer to the Creator, making him or her ever more similar to God, so that life may be lived in the image of God. In a nontheistic tradition like Buddhism, compassion brings its practitioner ever closer to freedom from clinging to the narrow confines of a self-centered way of being and opens a space for interconnection with all beings.

Love Thine Enemy

The beauty of the compassion-centered ethics within all the world's major religions is that it constitutes a path of spiritual self-development away from self-centeredness, which at the same time continually deepens one's grounding in a compassionate way of life. This process can be found in all the teachings—in some cases, perhaps more explicitly than in others. In the face of an act of harm done against oneself by another, for example, there is the initial stage where one does not respond in kind. This is the ethics of restraint. There is another stage, where one fully forgives the act done against oneself. And beyond the level of forgiveness, there is the possibility of an active generation of compassion or love for the perpetrator.

The principle is most beautifully captured in another famous saying of Jesus:

> You have heard that it was said, "Eye for eye, and tooth for tooth." But I tell you, Do not resist an evil person. If someone strikes you on the right cheek, turn to him the other also. And if someone wants to sue you and take your tunic, let him have your cloak as well. If someone forces you to go one mile, go with him two miles. Give to the one who asks you, and do not turn away from the one who wants to borrow from you. You have heard that it was said, "Love

your neighbor and hate your enemy." But I tell you: Love
your enemies and pray for those who persecute you.

(MATT. 5:38–44)

When I think of this passage from the Gospels, it reminds me of
an encounter I once had with a close colleague of mine, Lopön-la,
who was a monk at Namgyal monastery in the Potala Palace complex.
He had spent eighteen years in a Chinese prison after the fall of
Tibet in 1959, but was able to come to India in 1980. Since we had
known each other in Tibet, we occasionally had tea and a chat once
he got to India. During one of these conversations, quite casually,
Lopön-la said that there had been two or three occasions when he
felt in real danger. I naturally thought he was in fear for his life and
asked, "What kind of danger?" He answered, "The danger of losing
my compassion for the Chinese." When I heard this response, I simply bowed. It is not surprising that some among the Tibetan people
have turned to anger toward the Chinese communists who have de-
prived them of their country, freedom, livelihood, and traditional
spiritual practice. I myself have been roused to passion in response
to hearing terrible stories of abuse and tragedy from numerous Tibetans who have fled across the Himalayas. But the path of spiritual
perfection insists that to respond in this way only perpetuates the
cycle of suffering, as Buddhism would put it. The story of Lopön-la,
which I love to share, is an extraordinary testament that it is possible
to live by a compassion-centered ethics at the highest level, even in
the most trying of circumstances.

Few things are so difficult as what Jesus or the Buddha advocate:
to turn the other cheek so that one may be struck a second time, to
give one's cloak as well as one's coat, to go the second mile, to love
the enemy, to see the enemy as your spiritual teacher—to bless them

that curse you, do good to them that hate you, and pray for them that mistreat and persecute you. One might say that the entire spiritual path—all its exercises, abstinences, purifications—in every religious tradition has been created in order that, when put to the test of harm done against oneself, the practitioner can spontaneously respond with compassion. At the same time, the practicing of loving-kindness toward one's enemy is the ultimate test of one's own spiritual attainment. In his *Compendium of Training*, the great eighth-century Indian master Shantideva asks, "If you do not practice compassion toward your enemy, toward whom can you practice it?" The essence of the teaching that one should love one's enemy is this: if you can feel compassion for your enemy, then there is no limit to how far and how widely you can extend your compassion.

One reflection that arises from the agreement of all the major religious traditions on the centrality of compassion is that it reminds us of one of the most fundamental qualities of human nature. Because we have all been nurtured in a womb, because we are all born of a mother, affection is in our basic nature. From the loving caress of a mother's touch to the intimate connection with her breast as we suck, not only are we brought into being through love but also our young life is nourished and nurtured through love. Today, we know from science that the mother's simple physical touch plays a crucial role in the development of a child's brain in the first few weeks of life. It is in this affection that the preciousness of life is rooted; it is from this seed of affection that the great tree of compassion can grow.

To me, what makes our human species unique is not only that we are capable of imagining infinite altruism but also that we can actually experience it; not only can we bring it into being within ourselves, but we can also sing its praises to inspire others to do likewise. For instance, Shantideva writes:

This is the elixir of eternal life
That vanquishes the lord of death;
This is the limitless storehouse of treasure
That relieves poverty in the world.

This is the supreme medicine
That cures the sickness of beings;
This is the shade-giving tree
Where the weary on the path can rest.

This is the causeway that offers rescue
For sentient beings in the lower realms;
This is the rising moon of the mind
That softens the scorching of afflictive heat.

This is the great sun that dispels
The darkness of ignorance from the world;
This is the fresh butter extracted from
Churning the milk of sublime Dharma.

(BODHICARYAVATARA 3:28–31)

The beautiful thing about compassion is that when it spontaneously arises in you, an inner door opens onto that infant's experience of love, which is part of your fundamental reality. From a secular perspective, given our biological nature as social animals, nurturing is an integral part of the human survival mechanism. Here, too, without our mother's love and the infant's instinctive ability to seek and appreciate the mother's affection, we have no chance of survival. I often cite the evidence from medical science that demonstrates how simple physical touch by the mother, or another caregiver, is the most crucial factor in enlarging the physical size of our brain during the first few weeks after our birth. This shows how crucial the role of other people's love and compassion is for any person's survival and well-being. So, to feel compassion for another is, therefore, to return to our deepest nature. When the inner door opens it becomes effortless to reach out and connect with others. This is why the greatest antidote to insecurity and the sense of fear is compassion—it brings one back to the basis of one's inner strength. A truly compassionate person embodies a carefree spirit of fearlessness born of the freedom from egoistic self-concern. The quality of compassion is inborn, the inheritance of every human being; whether one is a believer or not, on this level there is no difference. What the teachings of the world's religions seek to do is help us recognize this heritage and provide us with a systematic means to foster it, enhance it, and bring it to perfection.

The Wisdom of Compassion

One very important element of the world's religious teachings on compassion is the dimension of metaphysical grounding. All the theistic religions repeatedly emphasize the love of God and the compassionate nature of His being. Acting from compassion is, therefore, understood to be a way of emulating, even imitating, God. This is why it is the perfect form of action. In Buddhism, the metaphysical dimension involves recognition of the deep intertwining nature of the self and others, as well as the understanding that, at the most basic level, we all share a deep aspiration to happiness and the wish to overcome suffering. In this context, the assumed independence of the self and others comes to be largely a false construct of the mind.

The great advantage of this metaphysical dimension—which in Buddhist language may be called the "wisdom aspect"—is that it grounds all our ethical actions in a foundation that is larger than the individual. The perspective is now universal rather than self-centered or reciprocal. In a theistic religious context, this would involve the deep understanding that everything that happens in the world, including suffering perpetrated upon oneself by others, exists within the dispensation of God's love and that God is infinite love. This is what grounds the ethic of turning the other cheek and loving the enemy.

The immense power of the theistic approach is that the believer can put aside his or her own immediate impulses to anger or revenge and—in service of that greater love of God which is the first commandment—turn the mind to a compassionate embracing of those who have treated others badly.

In Buddhism, which has no creator God, this practice entails a range of reflections. On the basic level, contemplation of the law of karma reminds us that one will reap the results of any action. On a deeper level, one reflects on the fundamental equality of self and others insofar as the basic aspiration for happiness and the avoidance of suffering is concerned; this sense of equality, together with a profound recognition of our shared sentient nature, inevitably prompts the flow of compassion. Within these practices, one might bring to mind thoughts of the utterly transient nature of all things, the teachings on no-self, and the deeply interdependent truth of everything. For example, when someone treats me in an unjust manner, instead of reacting with anger, I must ask "From what suffering does this action arise? What kind of afflicted mental states have taken over the perpetrator's mind? What habits and conditions propel him to act in this manner?" The result of placing the event—the harm done to me—within the space raised by these kinds of contemplations leads me to recognize that the appropriate response is not vengefulness, but compassion. Furthermore, within Buddhism there is the notion that there is only one task for fully enlightened beings—namely, to work tirelessly and selflessly for the good of others. This is their only aspiration, their only goal; and as a Buddhist if one wishes to please the Buddhas, this is the only deed that one must do. In the words of Shantideva,

> This alone is the propitiation of the Tathagatas;
> This alone is the fulfillment of my own goal;
> This alone beats back the sufferings of the world;
> So let this alone be my vow.
>
> (BODHICARYAVATARA 6:126–27)

Altruistic Action

The highest form of compassion, as a practice in daily life, is selfless service of others—in other words, pure altruistic action. Again, this quality is stressed in all the traditions. Whether it is presented as a direct injunction, in the form of a story or in a dialogue, the scriptures in the world religions exhort their followers to aspire to this ideal. In one of the most famous *Jataka Tales* (canonical stories of the Buddha's former births) in the Sanskrit tradition, the narrative depicts a young man who comes upon a starving tigress in a forest, who is so weak from hunger that she can no longer hunt and can survive only by eating her own newborn cubs. With spontaneous compassion, he offers himself as her meal; and since the tigress is too weak to attack him, he cuts himself open so that she can eat.

In the Gospels, Jesus tells the parable of the Good Samaritan, who finds a man by the roadside half dead, robbed, and ignored by passersby. The Samaritan, moved with compassion, bound up his wounds, put him on his own donkey, and brought him to an inn. He left him at the inn, giving the innkeeper money to look after him.

In the Talmud, it is written, " 'Ye shall walk after the Lord, your God,' but how can a man walk after God who is a devouring fire? It means, walk after his attributes: clothe the naked, visit the sick, comfort the mourner, bury the dead" (Talmud, Sota 14a). Similarly, in the *Pancastikaya-sara* by Jain monk Kundakunda, we read "Charity—to be moved at the sight of the thirsty, the hungry and the miserable, and to offer relief to them out of pity—is the spring of virtue" (137).

In Hinduism, there is a famous dialogue with the Voice of Thunder in the Upanishads, where the ethical process from restraint through to compassion is poetically encapsulated. When the gods, humans, and *asuras* (demi-gods) dwelt together as students and had finished their religious education, they asked God for a summary of what they had learned:

When they had completed their studentship, the gods said, "Teach us, father."
He spoke to them the syllable, DA. "Did you understand?"
"We understood," they said. "You told us, 'Be self-controlled.' "
"OM" he said. "You understood."

Then the human beings said to him, "Teach us, father."
He spoke to them the syllable, DA. "Did you understand?"
"We understood," they said. "You told us, 'Give.' "
"Yes!" he said. "You understood."

————

Then the asuras said to him, "Teach us, father." He spoke to them the syllable, DA. "Did you understand?"
"We understood," they said. "You said to us, 'Be compassionate.' "
"Yes!" he said. "You understood."

This is what the divine voice that is thunder, repeats, DA DA DA. "Be self-controlled! Give! Be compassionate!" One should practice this set of three, self-control, giving and compassion.

(BRHADARANYAKA UPANISHAD 5.2:2–3)

Here, the Hindu tradition offers, in one of its most revered and ancient scriptures, an incisive summary of the spiritual path of ethics from restraint to compassion.

In the modern world, there are many heart-lifting examples of such altruism. Regardless of how admirable the models of figures like Mother Theresa or Baba Amte may be, we should not think that altruistic action is uniquely the purview of such saintly beings. The potential for altruistic action lies in all of us, and it is possible on a daily basis for anyone. If one thinks of all the many ordinary people, religious and non-religious, who helped to save Jewish people during the Nazi era, many of these acts were performed purely out of altruistic motivation, where a key factor was the recognition of a shared humanity. But altruism lies in the simplest things: spontaneously helping an elderly or a blind person across the street, offering a seat on the bus or train to a mother with an infant, giving up one's place in a line to someone whose needs are more urgent. I am reminded of a picture I once saw, taken during the First World War, showing an Allied soldier nursing a wounded Turkish soldier, from the enemy side, during a break in the fighting. That is, as soon as the fighting stops, the two sides return to the human level in view of their shared suffering, and at that point they are able to empathize with the suffering even of an enemy.

It seems to me that, in this brief journey through the world's religions, we have discovered in their compassion-centered ethics a tremendous shared resource. If I am right about this, then, that resource is a wellspring for human goodness, with roots in every major culture and religious tradition. It turns, above all, on our recognition of shared humanity and universal human needs and aspirations, which are served by our basic human values. This suggests that, if we use the resources of religion by returning to this fundamental wellspring, the faith traditions can be an extraordinary source for good on this planet. It is the world's religions that can help overcome prejudices, deal with conflicts, and give succor to the poor and the weak.

This point was brought home to me in a practical way during one of my visits to Jerusalem. I met an Israeli teacher and a peace activist who used to run classes for Palestinian and Israeli children. Among other things, he taught that whenever you confront someone whom you dislike and who gives rise to fear or hostility in you, you should think of the image of God in that person's face. He told me the experience of a Palestinian student who had been to his courses and later came to see him. The student told him that, in the past, whenever he crossed an Israeli checkpoint, the sight of the soldiers caused him immediate anger and fear, but now that he practiced seeing the image of God in their faces, he no longer felt such emotional turmoil. Though this may not yet be the universal compassion that all religions hold up as the ultimate ideal, it is a remarkable and actual example of the compassionate turn away from hatred through a religious teaching.

8

A PROGRAM

FOR INTER-RELIGIOUS

UNDERSTANDING

The world's religions have often been a factor for division and conflict in the history of humanity. There is no denying that from
the Crusades in medieval times to jihad today, from the large-
scale Hindu-Muslim violence during India's partition in the mid-
twentieth century to the current Arab-Israeli conflict, and from the
Bosnian-Serb wars to the ongoing Sinhalese-Tamil fighting in Sri
Lanka—and not least the recent phenomenon of religion-inspired
global terrorism—differences in religions have been and continue to
be a sad factor of discord within the human family. Such conflicts
occur not only between religions but also between sects and factions
within any given religion, as the history of religious conflict in
Northern Ireland or the tragic antipathy of Shia and Sunni in Islam
show so clearly. Even within my own Tibetan tradition, sectarian attitudes and prejudices have created conditions of disharmony and

even actual conflict. In the face of this, the question still remains, "Does the diversity of the world's religions necessarily have to be a source of division in human society?"

While acknowledging this historical legacy, which is critical if we are to be serious about creating a genuine religious harmony, I believe that it is time to say that history is history and we must move on. I once told an audience of Muslim merchants and traders who are based in Bodh Gaya, the holy site of the Buddha's Enlightenment, that some of them may well be the descendants of the Islamic raiders who were responsible for the demolition of the Buddhist monasteries in India. But today—in new circumstances—there is a happy coexistence between Buddhist pilgrims and the Muslim merchants who provide them with restaurants and shops: the pilgrims enjoy the facilities and the merchants make a living from them. The point I am making is that historical memory cannot be allowed to stand in the way of living appropriately according to our new global reality, which demands peaceful coexistence.

I have always maintained that, if the world's religions are only a source of conflict and suffering, from the nontheistic point of view we humans should have the right to renounce them. But this is not the case. Yes, they have played a role in human division and conflict, but that need not be a necessary role, nor need it be the only role that religion can play. Each of the world's great religions has provided tremendous benefit to millions of human beings throughout its long history. In addition to offering the moral frameworks within which people can live their lives ethically, the religions have provided a deeper sense of meaning for millions of individuals, and they have also been a source of comfort and peace at times of personal tragedy and adversity. Today, despite the tremendous advances in science and technology, as well as the material developments these have given rise to, the world's great religions retain their relevance for humanity. I believe this situation will remain for at least a few more millennia, insofar as our basic human nature and condition remain the same.

So the critical question is not "Are religions only a source of trouble?" but, rather, "What can we do to ensure that the differences between religions do not continue to give birth to divisions and conflicts in human society?" Can the world's religions establish a genuine, lasting harmony between themselves? In dealing with religion and violence, I think it is important to distinguish between two distinct forms of conflict that have often been associated with religious differences. First, there are religiously affiliated conflicts where, although differences of religion may be a factor, the key issue is power, whether political, economic, ethnic, or institutional. Here, religious difference may cloak the dispute, but the fundamental problems concern disparities in wealth and power. This is particularly true of conflicts stirred up in the name of religion by people who are not themselves sincere. Second, there are conflicts that arise primarily as a result of differences in religious faiths, especially of doctrinal diversity. These participants are often sincere in their adherence to their own faiths; but this perspective, however sincere, results principally from a lack of contact with followers of other traditions and ignorance of the genuine value of traditions other than their own. A key remedy here involves broadening the horizons of one's knowledge and understanding. In the real world, the plurality of religious traditions is a fact of life—so, one way or another, we all need to learn to coexist with peace and harmony.

In themselves, differences are neither bad nor good, nor should they necessarily lead to conflict. It is how one deals with those differences that matters. Even within a single person's thoughts and emotions, he or she experiences all sorts of differences and contradictions—between earlier and later stages in life, even between what is felt and thought in the morning and later in the evening. In fact, it is in part these contradictory ideas and feelings that can give rise to new understanding and make us all more mature and insightful in relation to life and to the world.

Being a deep believer in the positive nature of human potential, I am committed to the view that genuine harmony between the world's great religions is achievable. However this can only be on the basis of promoting genuine understanding between the religions. Mutual understanding must rest on a solid foundation that includes, among other factors, an explicit recognition of the real differences that exist between the faiths. A successful approach cannot hide the differences by promoting some vague vision of all religions actually being one, nor can it be a syncretistic attempt to merge their various strengths into some universal faith. Rather, it must involve the explicit articulation and celebration of difference, for the differences between religions represent the beauty of God's infinite wisdom, (from a theistic perspective) and the richness of the human spirit. If inter-religious harmony is based upon a healthy recognition of the differences between faith traditions, this then allows us to transcend some of those differences and move beyond them to a higher level of convergence, where they share a common goal of human betterment and a set of key ethical teachings. At least, this is my own approach as I strive to promote inter-religious understanding and harmony, a task that I see as one of my most important missions.

So the question is how do we do it: How do we promote an inter-religious harmony based on mutual understanding and respect? In my own behavior, I have adopted several key practices. These include promoting greater contacts between followers of the world's different religions, especially at the grassroots level. To this end, wherever I travel, whether it is to a large metropolitan city or a small town, I am always keen to join an interfaith service. Here, I am using my being an outsider to encourage leaders and followers of local religious communities to get together. This brings an occasion for members of different faith traditions to share in each other's devotional services.

My program for the promotion of inter-religious harmony and understanding includes the following four key elements: (1) dialogue between scholars of religion on the academic level regarding the convergences and divergences of their respective faith traditions and—more important—the purpose of these different approaches; (2) sharing of deep religious experiences between genuine practitioners; (3) high-profile meetings of the religious leaders to speak and pray from one platform; and (4) joint pilgrimages to the world's holy places.

DIALOGUE BETWEEN SCHOLARS OF RELIGION ON THE ACADEMIC LEVEL

As a first step, it is vital to have some understanding of the key aspects of faith traditions other than one's own. This is especially critical if one is not to succumb to the easy option of believing that all religions are fundamentally one, or that even if they are not so at this stage, a truly universal religion will emerge eventually in the world. Often, ignorance of the "other" leads to suspicion and fear, which serve as the basis for distance and mistrust. Dialogue is especially helpful for highlighting the differences, above all on the doctrinal and philosophical level, between the different religions. For example, there is no denying the fact that, although most religions are theistic—the belief in a Transcendent Being as creator—there are others, such as Buddhism, Jainism, and one branch of ancient Indian religion known as Samkhya that are genuinely nontheistic. The difference between a belief in God and the absence of such a belief is a fundamental one; there is no point in pretending otherwise.

Within the Abrahamic traditions, there is a genuine doctrinal difference among the three about the status of Jesus Christ. For followers of Judaism, Jesus is not the Messiah promised in the Old Testament, while for Christians, Jesus is not only the promised Messiah or Christ but is, in fact the Son of God. As the Gospel puts it, "I am the Way, the truth and the life" (John 14:6), so for Christians, Jesus Christ is the Way as well as the Truth—in fact, God himself. For Islam, Jesus is a prophet but not the culmination. That is Muhammad, who is God's last prophet, and the Qur'an represents the culmination of God's final message to his creatures.

No benefit will come from denying that these are fundamental doctrinal differences among the three religions. The challenge is to find a way in which the followers of these traditions can, despite remaining true to their doctrinal standpoints, revere one another as representing legitimate paths to God. In my own case, even though my own faith tradition, Buddhism, is not theistic, nothing stops me from developing deep admiration and reverence toward the theistic teachings that provide so much inspiration and solace to so many of my fellow humans—and that have enabled the spiritual development of so many saints and spiritually evolved beings.

From the point of view of theistic traditions, Buddhism's lack of belief in God can seem somewhat unsettling. The idea of a religion with no place for God is, for many, a contradiction, or at best a paradox. But these issues can be clarified through open, scholarly discussion. The advantage of acknowledging the differences within the context of a scholarly discussion is that, given the descriptive nature of the discourse, there is no threat felt on the part of the partici-pants. Once there is a deeper appreciation of the divergences of doctrinal teachings, we can move on to ask the critical question of what may be the purpose of these different doctrinal views in the different traditions. All these views—despite their different content and context—share the same goal and purpose in promoting human happiness: a more compassionate humanity and grounding ethics. Such discussions are, therefore, tremendously helpful in drawing at-tention to the areas of convergence among the different faiths, espe-cially regarding how to live an ethical life.

DIALOGUE BETWEEN GENUINE PRACTITIONERS

One of the most effective methods of developing genuine apprecia-tion of other traditions is to share deep religious experiences. I re-member most vividly the impact of my meeting with a Christian hermit in the early 1980s, during a visit to Europe. As part of this trip I went to the ancient Benedictine monastery of Montserrat near Barcelona, which is situated in the mountains and has traditionally been a retreat for hermits. Nestled in the rocks, it reminded me of the remote hermitages that one finds in parts of Tibet. During my few days at this tranquil spot, a Christian monk came to see me. I was told that this fragile-looking father had spent five years as a her-mit in a cave behind the monastery. He was a Catalan who spoke very little English—in fact, I found that my rusty English was far better than his—so our conversation remained somewhat limited! (I later told others jokingly that because my English was better than his, I felt all the more bold to converse with him in English.) Anyway, I asked him, "I was told that you remained in the mountains as a her-mit for five years. What were you practicing?" Without hesitation, he said, "Meditation on love." When he said this, his eyes were moist

and there was such depth of feeling. Upon hearing his simple response and sensing his presence, I was deeply moved. We remained
silent for quite a while, with our eyes gazing into each other's, simply
feeling each other's presence. There was no need for any words. At
that moment silence spoke more than words. This had a profound
impact on me, especially with respect to the power of Christian contemplative practice.

My personal meetings with Hindu practitioners, such as Swami
Ranganathananda, have deepened my reverence for the efficacy of
Hindu teachings. Similarly, my longstanding friendship with the
Jain teacher Acharya Tulsi has truly convinced me of the tremendous depth of the Jain faith. On the Islamic front, one of the earliest
encounters I had with Muslims outside India took place during my
visit to Malaysia, where I was fortunate to join an inter-religious
meeting. Needless to say, it is my regular meetings with the Muslims
of Ladakh that have convinced me of the compassionate power of
Islam. My meetings with Jewish rabbis, especially those who are
practitioners of Kabbalah, such as Rabbi Zalman, have illuminated
the depth of the Jewish religious heritage for me.

When genuine practitioners from two different traditions meet,
they are able to recognize the qualities present in each other as the
very same qualities that they seek to cultivate in their own faith traditions, in the fashion of seeing one's own face in a mirror. Paradoxically, it is only when one has a deep experience rooted in one's own
faith tradition that one is able to appreciate the value of other religions. For without some experience grounded in one's own faith,
one simply does not have a point of reference with which to relate to
another's deep religious realization.

Many years ago I heard a heartwarming story. As part of an
ongoing Buddhist-Christian monastic exchange program, groups of
Tibetan Buddhist monks and nuns spent some time in various

Christian monasteries and nunneries in the United Kingdom and the United States. In return, groups of Christian monastics spent some time in the Buddhist monasteries and nunneries in the Tibetan communities in India. During one of these exchanges, some Benedictine monks visited Drepung and Ganden, two of the Tibetan monastic universities in southern India. In addition to participating in Buddhist rituals and ceremonies, participants held a two-day dialogue on comparative Christian-Buddhist monasticism. As the abbot of the Christian monastery began to describe the Rule of Saint Benedict, its origin and development, around a thousand Tibetan monks at this meeting were utterly surprised at the similarity between the Rule and the Buddhist monastic codes that they themselves live by. This was a truly eye-opening experience for many Tibetan monks, the majority of whom do not read or speak English and previously saw the Benedictines with their white sleeves and hooded robes as a very strange kind of monk. This single experience changed their perspective such that, from that point onwards, they were able to relate to Christian monks as fellow members of a monastic community.

MEETINGS BETWEEN THE LEADERS OF THE FAITHS

The third element in a systematic promotion of inter-religious harmony and understanding is the occasional, high-profile summits of world religious leaders. Here, I must acknowledge the profound contribution made by the late pope, His Holiness John Paul II, when he successfully convened the Inter-Religious Meeting of Prayer for Peace in Assisi, Italy, in 1986. At this meeting, attended by many of the world's religious leaders, we prayed from a single platform and for a single goal—namely, world peace—in a united voice. Not only was this historic, it was also deeply touching.

I remember the prayer session clearly to this day. It was a cold October morning and it had rained the night before. The stage was filled with religious leaders from all over the world, each in his own traditional habit—the Hindus in their characteristic saffron, the Jains in white, the Muslims with white caps or headwraps, the Jewish rabbis with their kippahs, the various Christian denominations in their different colored robes, a Japanese Zen priest in brown, myself in traditional Tibetan maroon, the chief patriarch of the Cambodian tradition in orange, and the African religious leaders in their native colorful cotton. The pope, in his pristine white papal robes, sat at the center with me to his left and the patriarch of the Greek Orthodox Church to his right, followed by the archbishop of Canterbury.

Thousands of ordinary people had turned up for the summit and, needless to say, there were large numbers of the world's media as well. At one point during the evening prayer session, I began to get concerned about one of the African religious leaders. He was wearing a white robe made of thin cotton, which may have been perfect for the tropical heat of Africa, but was disastrous in the cool autumn evening in Europe. I myself felt so cold that I had to wrap myself up, including my head, in my upper shawl-like robe. I kept looking at this African leader every now and then, hoping that someone would bring some blankets. After a while, the organizers did bring a blanket as well as a small heater to keep him warm. But by that time he was already shivering so badly that in the end he fell off his chair. Otherwise, the ceremony went smoothly. On that day, Assisi, a city closely associated with Saint Francis, who was a great proponent of universal peace and kinship, became truly a center of world peace.

A skeptic might argue that, given the differences and historical animosity between some of the religions, this kind of gathering has no real substance. I would challenge such a view. I think that a world religions summit of this sort has a powerful symbolic effect. The simple fact of our coming together and speaking from a shared platform set a strong example to millions of followers of the world's religions all over the world. It signaled the need to reach out to each other and to pray for the common human goals of peace and happiness. At the least, a high-profile and much publicized meeting like this serves as visual proof of the plurality of the world of religion. Although a small segment of his own Catholic Church criticized the pope for this historic inter-religious gathering, the majority of the millions of Catholics all over the world stood firmly behind the Pope. His Holiness displayed courageous leadership not only to the Catholic world but to humanity as a whole. On several occasions during my private meetings with John Paul II, I requested His Holiness to convene similar Assisi-type meetings of world religious leaders to focus on such pressing issues as poverty in the Third World, longstanding social and political injustices, and the freedom of religious beliefs.

JOINT PILGRIMAGES TO HOLY SITES

An important practice that we could adopt for promoting greater religious understanding and harmony is joint pilgrimages to the holy sites of different religions. I formally began this practice for myself in 1976 in India, when I visited and prayed at a Hindu temple, a mosque, a church, a Sikh guruduwara, and a Jain temple on the same day in Varanasi. The day culminated with an evening celebration on the banks of the Ganges. Since then, I have repeated this practice in different parts of India, most memorably with a visit to the famous Jama Masjid, the grand fourteenth-century mosque in Delhi, and to Kerala a few years ago, where I participated in the rites of Arti (Hindu worship) and Ganesh Yantra in a Hindu temple, sang hymns in a Christian church, and attended Muslim prayer in a mosque—all in the same day.

Over the years I have had the privilege to visit many of the world's holiest sites, some of them leaving a deep imprint on my mind. On one occasion, for example, I went to Lourdes, in southern France, not as a tourist but as a pilgrim. I drank the holy water, stood in front of Mary's statue, and thought that here, on this spot, millions of people find blessing or tranquillity. As I looked at the statue of Mary, deep admiration and appreciation for Christianity arose within me, simply because this image of Mary provides so much benefit to millions of people. The practical value of the help it offers is quite clear. I prayed, "May this holy site continue to serve millions of fellow humans in the future as well as now."

Ours was an inter-religious group composed of Christians, Buddhists, and Muslims, so we all stood for a few minutes of silent meditation in front of Mary's shrine. During this same trip to France I went to Toulouse, where I was shown the shrine of Thomas Aquinas, the great Dominican theologian and Christian philosopher, who wrote a vast compendium of the Catholic faith. I reflected on how similar his role was to that of Tsongkhapa, the great fourteenth-century philosopher and sage who founded the Geluk school. I was proud to lay a traditional Tibetan scarf on Aquinas' tomb. Later I went on a pilgrimage to the Virgin's shrine at Fatima, in Portugal. There I had a mysterious experience. After laying a Tibetan scarf beneath the statue and after a period of silent meditation, I turned to leave but looked back for the last time and, unless something was wrong with my eyes, I actually saw Mary smiling at me. I felt a powerful surge of profound experience at that instant.

Perhaps the most meaningful inter-religious pilgrimage for me was my first visit to Jerusalem. After several decades of trying, I was finally able to visit the holy city in 1994. I began with early morning prayer at the Wailing Wall, which is the last standing wall of the Second Temple, destroyed in 70 CE. There were already a few devout Jews praying there. My organizers had kindly arranged for me to have a maroon kippah that matched my robes. What was particularly moving was the sight of all the little scrolls of prayers that had been put into the cracks of this ancient wall. For a moment, what came to mind was my own Tibetan tradition of putting prayer stones and flags in the sacred landscape. Later in the morning, I visited the Church of the Holy Sepulcher, which is revered as the site of Christ's death and resurrection. Today, it is shared by, among others, the Greek Orthodox and Roman Catholic churches in Jerusalem. That afternoon I went to see the al-aqsa Mosque and the Dome of the Rock. This is the site where Muslims believe that the Prophet ascended into heaven. Today, the site comprises a beautiful mosque with a golden dome that, I am told, is managed by the royal family of Jordan, which represents an unbroken line of the Hashmite lineage that is traced back to the Prophet himself.

In reflecting on how this city of Jerusalem is so sacred to three of the world's great religions, and that these sites are physically so close to one another, it struck me that perhaps the great prophets of the three Abrahamic religions were trying to tell their followers something important about coexistence. I prayed that lasting peace and understanding among peoples take firm root in the Middle East, beginning with genuine peace between the Israelis and the Palestinians.

Several years later, I was invited to a series of Christian-Buddhist dialogues entitled the "Way of Peace," organized by the Christian Meditation Group headed by my friend Father Laurence Freeman and founded by the well-known Canadian contemplative Father John Main. We have held peace retreats in Florence, Italy, and twice in Northern Ireland. In exchange, I hosted a meeting in Bodh Gaya, the most sacred place for Buddhists throughout the world. Every day, for a period of three days, a group of us—Buddhist monks and nuns and Christian monks, nuns, and lay practitioners—sat under the Bodhi Tree. We discussed the meeting points of Buddhism and Christianity, and we joined together in hours of silent contemplation under the tree. On the final day, we were joined in our silent contemplative prayer by local Hindus, Jains, and Muslims. For many Buddhist pilgrims, the sight of Christian monks and nuns sitting in contemplation under the Bodhi Tree was amazing.

Recently, when I officiated in the consecration ceremony of a beautiful golden statue of the Buddha that was installed inside the Buddha Vihar complex in Gulbarga in Karnataka state, in southern India, I was touched to see that the organizers had used the occasion to host an inter-religious meeting. So the consecration was attended not just by Buddhists but also by Hindus, Muslims, and Jains. Thus, at the grassroots level, if followers of different religions invite those of other traditions to their religious festivals, this will help make members of each tradition familiar with the prayers and rites of the others.

My fellow Nobel Laureate and friend Archbishop Desmond Tutu has suggested that we add one more item to this list of four main elements promoting inter-religious understanding and harmony. He made me promise—archbishops can sometimes be persuasive!— that whenever I spoke of inter-religious harmony, I should mention his addition, too: Every now and then, the leaders of the world religions should speak out in a single voice on issues of urgent need, such as natural disasters and tragedies. I think this is extremely important advice.

My friend the Imam of Ajmer once suggested that I call a kind of United Nations of world religious leaders. In response, I shared with him my own more limited aspiration to see an association of religious leaders set up at national levels. For example, in India, such a group could act swiftly to intervene in any flare-up of religious conflict. Over the last several months, we have made significant progress toward setting up such an association of religious leaders and scholars in India. From my own personal experience, I can attest to the effectiveness of religious leaders speaking out forcefully in situations of communal conflict. Once, many years ago, there was a tragic conflict between Buddhists and Muslims in Ladakh, some even involving the burning of shops belonging to the other community. I personally intervened and pleaded both sides, especially writing letters to the community leaders, which really helped calm the situation and lay a foundation for a much more harmonious relationship between the two communities. Today, the relations between the two communities remain very good. One very attractive feature of the Muslim community in Ladakh is the amazingly close relation that exists between the Sunnis and the Shiites. In fact, on several occasions, I have made the suggestion to the Ladakhi Muslims that they send delegations to areas in different parts of the world where tensions, and sometimes actual conflicts, characterize the relationship between the two main communities of the same Islamic faith. By sharing their experience and historical example of peaceful coexistence, the Ladakhi Muslims can truly make an important contribution toward greater peace, harmony, and understanding between the Sunnis and the Shiites.

In response to my friend Imam's suggestion, over the last several months, we have made significant progress toward setting up such an association of religious leaders and scholars in India. Our plan is to meet in person every six months so that we keep close contact among ourselves and discuss many of the challenges we collectively face as members of world's great religions. These challenges include, among others, the relationship between the different faiths as well as with the religions and non-believers, the challenge of secularism, ethical issues raised by advances in science and technology, violence, conversion, and the environment. One very important consequence of this collaboration is to send powerful signals to lay members of the faith traditions to appreciate the need for and, more important, the value of inter-religious harmony and understanding.

On the global stage, the leaders of the world's religions can speak forcefully if their voices are united on a critical question, such as global warming. We can also speak powerfully against any violence committed in the name of religion. However, in order to do so, in a voice that is both credible and substantive, the world's faith traditions need to get their own acts together. The first step is to ensure that one's own faith tradition never becomes another force for conflict and suffering in the world. So the question is, "Is genuine harmony based on understanding ever likely to be achieved among the world's faith traditions?" I believe there is a real possibility. To achieve this, each faith tradition must address the question of how, in its deepest heart, it can truly accept the reality and full value of the other faith traditions. This is the challenge we must now address head on.

9

THE PROBLEM

OF

EXCLUSIVISM

The Challenge of "Other" Religions

For many religious people, accepting the legitimacy of other faith traditions poses a serious challenge. To accept that other religions are legitimate may seem to compromise the integrity of one's own faith, since it entails the admission of different but efficacious spiritual paths. A devout Buddhist might feel that acceptance of other spiritual paths as valid suggests the existence of ways other than of the Buddha toward the attainment of enlightenment. A Muslim might feel that acceptance of other traditions as legitimate would require relinquishing the belief that God's revelation to the Prophet, as recorded in the Qur'an, represents the final revelation of the highest truth. In the same vein, a Christian might feel that accepting the legitimacy of other religions would entail compromising the key belief that it is only through Jesus Christ that the way to God is found. So the encounter with an entirely different faith, which one can neither avoid nor explain away, poses a serious challenge to deep assumptions.

This raises these critical questions:

- Can a single-pointed commitment to one's own faith coexist with acceptance of other religions as legitimate?
- Is religious pluralism impossible from the perspective of a devout person who is strongly and deeply committed to his or her own faith tradition?

Yet without the emergence of a genuine spirit of religious pluralism, there is no hope for the development of harmony based on true inter-religious understanding.

Historically, religions have gone to great lengths, even waging wars, to impose their version of what they deem to be the one true way. Even within their own fold, religions have harshly penalized those heterodox or heretical voices that the tradition took as undermining the integrity of the inviolable truths that the specific faith represents. The entire ethos of missionary activity—that is, the focus on bringing about active conversion of people from other faiths or no faiths—is grounded in the ideal of bringing the "one true way" to those whose eyes remain unopened. In a sense, one might even say that there is an altruistic motive underlying this drive to convert others to one's own faith.

Given this history and, more important, given the perception of conflict that many religious people feel between maintaining the integrity of their own faith and the acceptance of pluralism, is the emergence of genuine inter-religious harmony based on mutual understanding possible at all? Scholars of religion speak of three different ways in which a follower of a particular faith tradition may relate to the existence of other faith traditions. One is a straight-forward *exclusivism*, a position that one's own religion is the only true religion and that rejects, as it were by default, the legitimacy of other faith traditions. This is the standpoint adopted most often by the adherents of the religious traditions. Another position is *inclusivism*, whereby one accords a kind of partial validity to other faith traditions but maintains that their teachings are somehow contained within one's own faith tradition—a position historically character-ized by some Christian responses to Judaism and Islam's relation to both Judaism and Christianity. Though more tolerant than the first position, this second standpoint ultimately suggests the redundancy of other faith traditions. Finally, there is *pluralism*, which accords va-lidity to all faith traditions.

True Acceptance of the "Other's" Reality

It is understandable, given the seemingly irreconcilable conflict be-tween commitment to one's own faith and a true embracing of reli-gious pluralism, that many people feel that genuine inter-religious understanding and harmony requires the acceptance of some kind of ultimate unity of all religions. Citing the metaphor of multiple rivers all converging into the great ocean, some suggest that the world's faith traditions, with their distinct doctrinal beliefs, and practices all ultimately lead to the same place. For instance, that place may be union with the Godhead, regardless of however differently this God-head may be referred to—Jehovah, God, Ishvara, Allah, and so on.

My own view is different. The possibility of genuine inter-religious understanding and harmony should not be, and need not be, contingent upon proving the ultimate oneness of all religions. The problem with such an approach is that it demands a precondition that remains impossible for the majority of adherents of the world's great religions. In fact recognition of diversity among the world's faiths is not only essential but also the first step toward creating deeper understanding of each other. True understanding of the "other" must proceed from a genuine recognition of and respect for the other's reality. It must proceed from a state of mind where the urge to reduce the other into one's own framework is no longer the dominant mode of thinking.

To begin, whether we like it or not, the existence of other religions is an undeniable fact. It is also undeniable that the teachings of the great religions provide great benefits to their adherents. Even the Buddha failed to turn the entire population of central India into Buddhists, let alone the entire world. Hinduism, too, failed to convince a significant proportion of the population of the Indian subcontinent of the primacy of the Vedic way to *moksha* (salvation). Similarly for Christians, Jesus did not convert the entire population of the holy land into his followers—nor did he try to. From the point of view of Islam, even after the Prophet's appearance in the world, the presence of Jews and Christians remained an inalienable part of the landscape of the Middle East.

It is impossible for the 6 billion human inhabitants of our planet to all follow the same religion. First, the diversity of mental dispositions, spiritual inclinations, and different kinds of conditioning has always been a basic feature of human society, and one set of spiritual teachings would simply not serve everyone. Second, given the long history of the religions—in some cases, stretching over thousands of years—they have evolved in a complex human geography adapted to specific cultural sensibilities and environments, giving rise to different habits of mind. Such things cannot be changed overnight, nor is it desirable that they be. So creating a single religion for the world, whether a new one or one of the old ones, is simply unfeasible.

Especially in today's globalized world, where not only nation to nation but even continent to continent our fates are deeply intertwined, the acceptance of the reality of other faiths is critical for the sake of peace and human happiness. Furthermore, because of modern communication, tourism, and the global economy, the world's religions are in daily contact with one another. The era when a particular faith could exist in the comfort of isolation is gone forever. Given this new reality of our world, the only alternative left to religious pluralism is an increasing sense of division and conflict. So, in brief, the standpoint of religious exclusivism represents a perspective that is not in accord with reality.

From the point of view of a religious person who seeks to live his or her life according to the dictates of a sound ethical way of life, it becomes especially incumbent upon us to accord deep reverence to all faith traditions. In the past these traditions have provided inspiration, meaning, and ethical guidance to millions of people. Today, too, despite tremendous advances in the field of material development and human knowledge, these faith traditions continue to provide solace to millions of our fellow human beings. And in the foreseeable future, these traditions will continue to be a source of deep spiritual inspiration to millions.

Regardless of how one may feel about the specific doctrines of other faith traditions, this fact alone—their service to millions of fellow human beings—makes them worthy of our deep respect. Their profound benefit to others is really the ultimate reason each of us, believers and nonbelievers alike, must accord deep respect to the world's great faith traditions. For a believer, a key element here is to be truly sincere about the values of compassion that are at the heart of one's own faith tradition. For the ultimate reason to accord respect to other religions is to see that they, too, engender the beautiful qualities of the human heart and foster compassion and loving kindness—exactly the qualities one is striving to attain through one's own faith.

Interestingly, when it comes to actual spiritual practices, which I consider to be the essence of these religious teachings, as opposed to metaphysical or theological formulations, there is profound convergence across all traditions. All carry the message of love, compassion, and universal brotherhood and sisterhood. Based on these virtues, all teach forgiveness, forbearance, contentment, simplicity of life, and self-discipline.

Three Key Aspects of a Faith Tradition

In addressing the question of the plurality of religion, personally I find it helpful to draw a distinction between what can be seen as three key aspects of a religion: (1) ethical teachings, (2) doctrines or metaphysics; and (3) cultural specifics, such as attitudes to images. The first aspect pertains to the practitioner's daily life, whereby he or she needs to live according to the dictates of an ethics based on compassionate consideration of others' welfare. Essentially, this provides a guideline to the devout on how to live according to the spiritual ideals one espouses within the context of a society. In contrast, the second aspect of religion pertains primarily to its understanding of the ultimate truth, which is inevitably related to what happens to the believer in the afterlife. It is this second aspect that provides the rationale for the teaching on ethics and religious practice that makes up the first aspect. The third aspect, which is often bound up with cultural and historical circumstances, determines how believers may behave at a given place and time.

Once this distinction is drawn, the question of how to deal with the challenge posed for the devout by the plurality of religion assumes a different form. For example, on the level of ethical teachings, as I have shown in greater detail in the chapter on compassion, there is undeniably a great convergence of the world's great religions. The central message of all these religions is love, compassion, and universal brotherhood and sisterhood. Their presentations may be different—for example, a theistic tradition may admonish its followers to "love thy neighbor" as the wish of God, while a nontheistic tradition may say that, given the law of cause and effect, if one does not wish ill for oneself one should then refrain from doing ill to others. But on this level, the purpose of all religions remains the same: to contribute to the betterment of humanity, to create a more compassionate and responsible human being. Not only are the ethical teachings of the religions essentially the same, the fruits of love and compassion are the same as well. For example, just as Mother Theresa of Calcutta was a product of Christianity's great teachings on compassion, so too a great soul like Mahatma Gandhi (who demonstrated the power of nonviolence as an effective political means) was primarily a product of India's great religion, Hinduism.

Now, on the metaphysical and cultural levels—our second and third aspects of a religion—clearly there are differences among the religions, some of which are in fact quite fundamental. In the cultural domain, time and historical context may even cause significant differences within a given religion, as in the relatively recent espousal of women priests in the Anglican Church or in the differences between Buddhism in its traditional homelands—for instance,

Thailand, Sri Lanka, Japan, and Tibet. But the fundamental arena of difference lies in the second—doctrinal or metaphysical—aspect. For where a religion's doctrines play an active role, the distinctness of the faith traditions becomes most pronounced.

To begin with, even on the basic question of what happens in the afterlife, as well as the origins of the universe, there is much divergence. There is also a difference in the way in which the notion of well-being in this afterlife is defined. Lastly, there are differences in the method—the "path" in the Buddhist language—on how to realize this future well-being. Given these differences, it is no surprise that there are fundamental differences in the conception of what constitutes ultimate truth. Any attempt to find convergence on this doctrinal and metaphysical level is like the well-known Tibetan proverb, "trying to attach a yak's head on a sheep's body." The question, then, becomes what is the purpose of these different doctrinal and philosophical views? Here, I find a historical model from my own Buddhist tradition to be most helpful.

A Buddhist Hermeneutical Principle

Divergence of doctrinal and philosophical standpoints has always been an important part of Buddhism's own self-understanding. Soon after the Buddha's passing away, his followers evolved into distinct schools, each espousing somewhat different doctrinal and philosophical standpoints. Each of these teachings are based on the words of the Buddha, which means that one and the same teacher taught divergent—in some cases, in fact, contradictory—views of reality to his followers. For example, although the standard Buddhist doctrinal standpoint rejects the notion of an independent self, there is also a *sutra* where the Buddha states that the physical and mental constituents of a person are the burden while the person is the bearer of that burden, thus suggesting the presence of an agent independent of the physical and mental elements that make up a person's existence.

Similarly, there is a statement by the Buddha that karmic actions and their fruits exist, while in general the self that is thought to be the agent of the action and the experiencer of the fruits of the karmic action does not exist. There are also statements in which the Buddha rejects the reality of the external material world but affirms the existence of the world of consciousness. Finally, there are scriptures that reject any notion of the substantial existence of things, both material and mental. Here, then, the Buddha teaches all things to be empty of any substantial reality and that they exist only within the context of interrelated events of cause and effect. In technical Buddhist language, all conditioned things are impermanent and all things and events are dependently originated, thus lacking any objectively identifiable essence that defines their real existence.

Since all of these divergent, even contradictory, teachings were taught by the same teacher, does this mean that the Buddha himself was confused when it came to defining the ultimate nature of reality? Or, does this mean that the Buddha deliberately wished to create confusion in the minds of his followers? Clearly, for a devout Buddhist, both of these alternatives remain unacceptable. Furthermore, the fully awakened Buddha is, for the Buddhists, the embodiment of compassion for all things living—"a great friend even to those who are unacquainted," as a classical text puts it. So, how then are the followers of the Buddha to understand his divergent teachings? This is where the role of hermeneutics comes in.

———

The principle invoked by Buddhists in attempting to interpret the Buddha's conflicting teachings has to do with the understanding that what the Buddha taught is contingent on the needs of a given context and its potential for efficacy. In a sense, the Buddha, as teacher, did not have free reign on what to teach. His teaching, the Dharma, was a cure for the ailments of the spirit, aimed to awaken it to its highest perfection; therefore, it demanded adjustment to the specific context in which it was being taught. In a sense, the Dharma is a medicine whose effectiveness can be judged only in relation to the treatment of an illness. Since there are so many diverse mental dispositions, or spiritual and philosophical inclinations, among human beings, there should be equally corresponding numbers of teachings. The idea that there should be only one teaching—a kind of panacea that is valid for all beings—from this point of view is untenable.

For some, the idea that this very life has been created by God is deeply inspiring and also most powerful in providing a spiritual anchor; while for others, the notion of an all-powerful creator is troubling and even untenable. For some, the idea that what we are today is the result of our own past karma and what we will become is determined by how we live today is appealing and beneficial, while others find the idea of future lives and previous births incomprehensible. In fact, if the Buddha were to teach the doctrine of no-self to someone whose mental disposition is such that he or she is likely to understand this in nihilistic terms—as denying the very existence of a person, who is responsible for his or her intentional actions— not only would this be most unskillful on the Buddha's part but, more important, the teaching would be harmful for that person. In fact, to give the teaching of emptiness to someone whose mind is not ready for it is a direct infraction of one of the bodhisattva precepts.

In the case of prescribing medicine, a skilled physician will take into account the specific physical constitution of the patient, his age, fitness, proneness to negative reactions to certain substances, and so on. Depending on this, the physician will prescribe the medicine. Even with respect to one and the same patient, a skilled physician needs to be sensitive to how the patient responds to the dose, as well as different compositions of the medicine, so he can adjust both the dose and the composition as the patient progresses along the path of healing. In the same manner, a skilled spiritual teacher adapts his or her teachings, always maintaining deep sensitivity to the specific needs of a given situation. Therefore, a Buddhist cannot say, when relating to the Buddha's teaching, "this is the best teaching," as if one can make such evaluations independent of the specific contexts.

I often speak of a "supermarket of religions." Just as a supermarket rightly takes pride in its rich and diverse resources of food commodities for sale, in the same manner the world of religions can take pride in its rich diversity of teachings. Now, as for the question of why some people find certain religious teachings more appealing and effective than others, while different individuals have a negative reaction to the same teaching, from the Buddhist and classical Indian religious and philosophical points of view, it has largely to do with the person's own conditioning, including his or her karma. From a theistic perspective, it is a matter of God's mysterious workings. This is, in fact, the key reason I personally advise people to stay within their own traditional faith.

Personally, I find this hermeneutic principle most helpful when relating to the question of other religions, for it explains the value and richness of the great diversity of religions. Each religion, because of a long historical development that involved the experiences of so many generations, has its own beauty, logic, and uniqueness. Most important, this diversity enables the world's religions to serve such a vast number of human beings. In contrast, if there were only one historical religion, not only would the world be impoverished, especially in relation to its spiritual resources and imagination, but also that religion would fail to serve the needs of many people.

Seen from this angle, the diversity of religion becomes not an awkward problem; rather, it becomes an adornment of the human spirit and its long history. It is something to be celebrated rather than bemoaned. Understood thus, the urge to convert others to one's own faith loses its force. In its place arises a genuine acceptance of the reality of other faith traditions. Then, instead of seeing others as an aberration, or at worst as a threat, one can relate to others out of a sense of deep appreciation for their profound contributions to the world.

The Problem of Fundamentalism

Now, one possible response that a faith tradition can make in the face of the plurality of faiths, which is an inescapable fact of the contemporary world, is to embrace fundamentalism. This is, in fact, what many followers of religion have chosen to do. At its heart, fundamentalism is a reaction to a perceived threat to the integrity of one's own religious tradition. Just as we see fundamentalism in the Abrahamic religions, we also see fundamentalism in Asian religions such as Buddhism and Hinduism.

Broadly speaking, the fundamentalists, irrespective of their specific religious affiliation, tend to believe that the contemporary world is rife with immorality and ungodly values, and that the role of the devout is to try to bring human society back to a golden age when the world functioned according to the dictates of a moral God. In their quest for this goal, fundamentalists on the whole believe strongly that their scripture contains the totality of all the truths that are worth knowing, and that it is their responsibility to defend the truths of this scripture against the onslaught of pluralistic or secular ideas that inevitably relativize truth. An important part of the standpoint of fundamentalism is, therefore, to defend the literal truth of scripture and maintain its definitive status. For the fundamentalists, then, the commands of God as they understand them to be revealed in scripture are absolute, atemporal, and nonnegotiable.

Although fundamentalism need not necessarily lead to religious extremism, the line dividing the two remains a fine one. There is, however, one concern that underlies the fundamentalist standpoint, which pluralists need to take seriously. This is the concern that religious pluralism involves relativizing doctrinal truths. Here, if we invoke the distinction I made earlier of the three key aspects of a religion—ethics, doctrine, and culture—we can respond to this concern effectively. While allowing openness to interpretation in matters of practice and culture, which in any case pertain to guidelines for living within a society, even a religious pluralist can accept that the doctrines of his own scripture that primarily pertain to ultimate truth are definitive. In other words, one can be a religious pluralist yet maintain, for oneself, the doctrinal aspects of one's own tradition as representing the definitive truth.

Reconciling "One Truth, One Religion" with "Many Truths, Many Religions"

So, with these considerations as background, how does a follower of a particular religious tradition deal with the question of the legitimacy of other religions? On the doctrinal level, this is a question of how to reconcile two seemingly conflicting perspectives that pertain to the world's religious traditions. I often characterize these two perspectives as "one truth, one religion" versus "many truths, many religions." How does a devout person reconcile the perspective of "one truth, one religion" that one's own teachings appear to proclaim with the perspective of "many truths, many religions" that the reality of the human world undeniably demands?

As many religious believers feel, I would agree that some version of exclusivism—the principle of "one truth, one religion"—lies at the heart of most of the world's great religions. Furthermore, a single-pointed commitment to one's own faith tradition demands the recognition that one's chosen faith represents the highest religious teaching. For example, for me Buddhism is the best, but this does not mean that Buddhism is the best for all. Certainly not. For millions of my fellow human beings, theistic forms of teaching represent the best path. Therefore, in the context of an individual religious practitioner, the concept of "one truth, one religion" remains most relevant. It is this that gives the power and single-pointed focus of one's religious path. At the same time, it is critical that the religious practitioner harbors no ego-centric attachment to his faith.

Once at a conference in Argentina, the well-known Chilean scientist Humberto Maturana, who incidentally was a teacher of a close scientist friend of mine, the late Francisco Varela, said that, as a scientist, he should not be attached to his field, for this would obstruct his ability to study it with objectivity. This, I think, is an important insight that we in the religious world should also embrace. It means that I, as a Buddhist, must not feel ego-centric attachment to my own faith of Buddhism, for doing so obstructs me from seeing the value of other traditions.

In the context of society, however, the concept of "many truths, many religions" not only becomes relevant but also necessary. In fact, where there is more than one person, already the pluralistic perspective of "many truths, many religions" becomes critical. Thus, if we relate these two seemingly contradictory perspectives to their differing contexts of society and the individual we can see no real conflict between the two.

This still leaves unanswered the question of how we should relate to the divergent and contradictory doctrinal teachings of the religions. From the Buddhist point of view, the belief in a Transcendent God, with its emphasis on the idea of a first cause that in itself is uncaused, amounts to falling into the extreme of absolutism, a view that is understood to obstruct the attainment of enlightenment. In contrast, from the monotheistic religions' point of view, Buddhism's nonacceptance of God and divine creation amounts to falling into the extreme of nihilism, a view that is dangerously close to an amoral and materialistic view of the world.

But, on the other hand, from the theistic religions' point of view, if one believes that the entire cosmos, including the sentient beings within it, is a creation of one all-powerful and compassionate God, the inescapable consequence is that the existence of faith traditions other than one's own are also God's creation. To deny this would imply one of two results: either one rejects God's omnipotence— that is to say, that although these other faiths are false ways, God remains incapable of stopping their emergence—or, if one maintains that although God is perfectly capable of preventing the emergence of these "false" ways, He chooses not to do so, then one rejects God's all-embracing compassion. The latter would imply that, for whatever reasons, God chose to exclude some—in fact, millions of His own children—and left them to follow false ways that would lead to their damnation. So the logic of monotheism, especially the standard version that attributes omnipotence, omniscience, and all-embracing compassion to God, inevitably entails recognition that the world's many religious traditions are in one way or another related to God's divine intentions for the ultimate well-being of His children. This means that, as a devout follower of God, one must accord respect, and if possible, reverence to all religions.

From the Buddhist point of view, given the tremendous diversity among sentient beings, each individual and group with a long history of inclinations and propensities, people find different ways of approach more suited to their own spiritual inclinations and thus more effective for their spiritual development. This alone is adequate ground to develop a sense of appreciation of all faith traditions. From the liberal democratic point of view too, so long as one subscribes to the ideal that each citizen of a nation must be respected in his or her own right, one is also bound by this principle to respect the faith traditions that these individuals perceive to be the basis of their understanding of who they are as persons.

Given the need for upholding the perspective of "many truths, many religions" in the context of wider society, while the dictates of one's own faith demand embracing the "one truth, one religion" perspective, I believe that a creative approach is called for here—if one wishes to uphold both of these perspectives with integrity.

One might, for instance, make a distinction between *faith* and *respect* as two distinct psychological attitudes in relation to the world's religions. Faith is associated with such psychological states as cognitively oriented "belief," as well as more affectively oriented "trust" and "confidence." In contrast, respect is associated with appreciation and reverence, deriving particularly from the recognition of the values and importance of the object for which one has respect.

In the context of religion, then, faith pertains to truth—especially doctrinal truths—as proposed by one's own religion. Therefore, for a devout religious person, it becomes important to reserve faith for his or her own religion, while cultivating respect—in fact, deep reverence—for other religions. In the Sanskrit Buddhist tradition, a distinction is made between three types of faith *(shradda):* faith in the form of admiration, in the form of conviction, and in the form of emulation. Of these, admiration—the first form of faith—is effectively equivalent to respect or reverence, which as we have noted, can be fully extended to other religions.

There are two broad arguments for this idea of respect for other traditions. The first is the undeniable fact that, as mentioned earlier, these traditions have provided solace and spiritual development, as well as a laudable system of ethics, for millions of people and will continue to do so in the foreseeable future. The second, perhaps stronger, argument is that despite the doctrinal differences between religions (which cannot be bridged), just as the doctrinal teachings of my own faith admirably inform the ethical way of life of my own faith, so the doctrines of other faiths inform no less valid ethical ways of life in the other religions. The doctrines themselves cannot be reconciled, but the way they make it possible to ground strikingly parallel and praiseworthy ethical systems is a wonderful fact. This fostering of deep and active respect for other faith traditions is certainly doable, and it is how I practice myself.

10

THE

CHALLENGE

AHEAD

If I am right about the possibility for harmonious coexistence among the world's religions, three important consequences follow. First, the adherents of the world's great religions have it genuinely within their power to ensure that religion will never again be a source for discord or a cause of conflict in our human family. Second, while admitting our metaphysical differences, if we can truly appreciate that compassion is our collective and fundamental spiritual value, then we can speak with one voice. That is, we can genuinely act together as a force for goodness, harnessing the huge power and energy of millions of believers to the cause of peace and human happiness. Third, and most important but perhaps most difficult, is if we can agree that one of the most urgent tasks for humankind today is to establish genuine peaceful coexistence among peoples throughout the world, then the world's religions have a crucial role to play. Here, world religions can learn something from democratic politics. If different political parties advocating strikingly different views, and even underlying ideologies, can coexist within a political system and be united in their service to society, why can't the world's religions do the same? A whole-hearted embracing of pluralism, based on a respectful acceptance of each other's religions, is a prerequisite to achieving this. This is most difficult for two reasons, however. First, the goal of world peace is elusive; and second, the challenge is not just that the adherents of the faith traditions accept each other, as well as those without religion, but also that the secularists accept people of faith.

Religion and Violence

In light of religion's historical association with conflict and division, it is crucial that every major faith tradition acknowledge that it has served—and continues to have the potential to serve—as a factor for division, conflict, and suffering. This admission needs to be made through a critical process of self-education, so that the adherents of any given tradition remain vigilant against chauvinism, intolerance, bigotry, and violence. It is essential that the leaders of the world's religions—both local and international—make and reiterate regularly categorical statements against any use of their faith as justifications for violence. This must be understood and, as far as possible, practiced by individuals and congregations. Clearly, some aberrant groups and individuals may take it upon themselves to commit terror in the name of anything they fancy. But it is in the interests of all adherents of the faith traditions (not to speak of the world as a whole) to stand firm against violence and to insist that their voices not be hijacked by such extremists.

In understanding the association of religion with violence, it is important to distinguish among several factors. First, exclusivism itself—that of a chauvinistic position in regard to one's own faith—can be a primary cause of discord. Second, as I have mentioned earlier, often what seems like religious violence is, in fact, the product of complex historical, social, political, and economic conditions. What enables both of these causes of violence is the adoption of a faith tradition as an identity label that, instead of being a spiritual path to one's humanity, becomes a marker by which one defines oneself as opposed to others. The appropriation of religion as an identity label leads to a situation whereby, to use a classical Buddhist expression, the medicine itself is turned into a poison. The primary purpose of religious teachings is to tame the mind and open the heart. However, often the followers of a given faith inject the teachings with pollutions of their own negative impulses, with the result that the teachings close the heart and inflame the unruly mind. At that point, religion becomes a source of attachment and aversion, resulting in greater division, conflict, and delusion. Therefore, the key task of those responsible for leading their faith traditions is to guard against this. The teachings of one's faith, instead of being a justification for violence, should be an antidote to any violent tendencies latent in one's mind.

The challenge here is profound. The fact is that all the major religions explicitly emphasize compassion and regard for one's fellow humans—brothers and sisters, children of one and the same God, mother sentient beings, to use some of the language from different traditions. Yet, the history of inter-religious relations is fraught with conflict and discord. Clearly, there is something missing. While speaking of human beings as God's children, people forget the meaning of this when it comes to followers of different traditions. Buddhists may speak of all as mother sentient beings, but they ignore this when they relate to members of other faiths. So where does this disconnect come from?

Deeply, on the level of the individual practitioner, there needs to be the will to integrate the teachings into one's daily life. We need to allow our hearts to be softened by the very essence of our separate faith traditions. Those of us who have chosen a spiritual path have accepted the high bar of our faith's moral injunctions, and we must live in a way that is consistent with this commitment. To choose a religious path is a matter of personal preference, but once we have done so, it becomes incumbent upon us to follow it fully, consistently, and with integrity. In other words, we should be serious about our commitment to a faith. If, in contrast, the teachings of our religion do not play any significant role in our daily life, then frankly we have no religion, whatever claims we may make.

On the most down-to-earth level, we religious believers owe it to humanity to ensure that our own faith tradition ceases to be a cause of conflict or disharmony in the world. This is the least contribution we can make, for the sake of world peace. In this regard, there is the sensitive matter of proselytizing and conversion. I understand that in Christianity and Islam, it may be argued that a call to conversion is implicit for the believer; however, it is essential that these faiths recognize that religious conversion must always be freely embraced, with no imposition or bribe.

In today's globalized world, where all the major religions live in such close proximity, the practice of proselytizing, especially the more aggressive and insensitive kinds, leads to unnecessary tensions and the potential for conflict. Recognizing this, when I am asked to teach Buddhism in the West, I always remind people that their traditional religious heritage is Judeo-Christian and that, in general, it is better for people to remain within their inherited faiths. Similarly, I tell people in traditionally Buddhist countries like Mongolia that it is better for them to continue to uphold their inherited faith rather than convert. Given that faiths have evolved over a long time and within particular historical, cultural, and social environments, usually the local concepts and teachings are more suited to the spiritual inclinations and dispositions of the majority of people in the culture. There are, of course, always exceptions. But even if, after a long self-examination, one comes to adopt a new path, it is essential to resist the tendency to justify one's change of faith by becoming overly critical of or negative about one's religious heritage.

A Force for Good

In regard to the welfare of the wider world, the role of the world's religions is not confined to the cessation of discord rooted in their differences. Out of a common ground of compassion-based ethics, the major religions, as institutions and as communities of personally committed individuals, have great potential to act together positively for good. There is no denying that faith can be a powerful motivating factor, driving the believer to superhuman efforts. In the words of Saint Paul "faith can move mountains."

The power of religion as a motivating force lies in its special appeal to the whole range of the human psyche, including most importantly our emotions, against the backdrop of a vision of ultimate truth, with its provision of meaning and purpose. The time has come to channel this force so that it is directed toward meeting the many needs and challenges that humanity faces today. Clearly, to do this, the religions must get their act together by renouncing exclusivism, endorsing compassion as the central spiritual principle, and, above all, actively living that compassion through the practices of the individual believer.

Among the challenges immediately before us are the need to confront division between peoples based on prejudice, the crisis of the environment, the terrible inequities of poverty, and the ethical dilemmas posed by new scientific knowledge and technological innovations. The fact that religion has so often served as the ground for discord offers us the basis for understanding how differences, if not handled wisely, can result in conflict. In the case of Northern Ireland, for example, which I got to know a little after attending several interfaith peace meetings there, it was only after the main protagonists sat down to discuss their differences in a spirit of reconciliation and diminished exclusivity that it became possible to address the underlying social, political, and economic causes that had manifested as religious violence.

If we can harness the extraordinary resources that the faith traditions offer, problems such as racial and religious prejudice can be alleviated and perhaps even overcome. For example, what can be more potent in countering prejudice than the genuine, heartfelt conviction that all humans are children of one and the same Father in heaven? Historically, one of the strengths of the world's religions is that each encompasses a wide range of ethnicities and geographical locations among its adherents. What is needed is to expand on this without excluding anyone, whether members of other religions or nonbelievers. In essence, by using the force of their own religious teachings, the faithful can learn to relate to the whole of humanity as a collective "we." Indeed, when massive disasters strike, like the 2004 Indonesian tsunami, we spontaneously respond with collective humanity. What we need is a way of sustaining this collective human consciousness, as well as the acts of compassion that stem from it, so that we can effectively rise to such challenges as global warming, the growing scarcity of natural resources, and the need for lasting peaceful coexistence.

One area where followers of the world's major religions have a role to play is the crisis facing the environment. Simply put, for our planet to survive we need fundamental change, both in our behavior and in our underlying outlook with respect to nature. In both of these arenas, I see an effective role for the world's faith traditions.

On the level of our behavior, unless we humans as a species can learn to exercise significant restraint in our lifestyles, as well as in our consumption of natural resources, frankly there is very little hope. The faith traditions, all of which emphasize a life of simplicity on the personal level and a need for moderation in our desires, offer a real ground on which such radical behavioral change can take place. Moreover, the emotional and rational power of religion is, in fact, what is needed to galvanize us to make these adaptations in our lifestyle. Imagine the impact of such a gesture from the followers of Christianity, Islam, and Hinduism! Among them, there are more than a billion human beings—a hugely significant proportion of the world's population. The heroes of the world's religions—from their founders to countless saints, as well as holy men and women—whose biographies we may take to represent the paradigms of religious living, all exemplify simplicity and moderation of desire.

On the level of transforming our worldview in relation to the environment, religion's collective vision of the earth as the mother that sustains us—the container-world with which we are karmically connected according to Buddhism, the ground that the Creator made in which to place us from a theistic viewpoint—can have a deeply transformative effect if we can grasp this wisdom fully. Here, we have something genuine to learn from the indigenous spiritual traditions — above all, in the connection of an ethical religious life with a proper and compassionate relationship to the environment. For many of these traditions, the earth and its well-being are central concerns in ways that are becoming crucial to all inhabitants of our planet. For example, the Hopi Indians of the southwestern United States, whose elders I have met several times, conceive of the cosmos in terms of the earth, whom they venerate as "our mother" — the upper world and the underworld from which the Hopi came and to which their spirits go after death. The respect for Mother Earth is a central part of rituals that include dances among numerous tribes, from the Pueblo Indians to the Sioux, in the United States and Canada, as well as native peoples in Central and South America. Similar reverence can be found among the Maori and Polynesian peoples, who venerate the Earth-Mother and the Sky-Father as their ancestors. Again, the reverence for nature occupies great importance in the beliefs and rites of Japanese Shinto practice. Whenever I have the chance to participate in a native ritual, with its incense, dances, and invocation of Mother Earth, I am moved by the vision of existence that embraces the deep interdependence of human beings, animals, and nature.

As an example of religious commitment to the environment, I particularly wish to applaud the efforts of the Greek Orthodox Patriarch Bartholomew I, who has taken it upon himself to promote the message of caring for our natural world as an essential precept of being a good Christian. Linking faith and ecology, the patriarch argues that to commit a crime against the natural world is no different from committing a sin. This is a beautiful example of how a religious leader can bring his faith tradition into the wider service of humanity, where living a religious life according to one's own faith comes to

attain a significant global dimension. I have no hesitation in echoing
this message as a call to all my fellow Buddhists to do the same. I
know of some Thai monks who wrapped their yellow robes around
trees so that villagers and loggers were reluctant to cut them down.
This is an example of using people's regard for the Dharma as a
means of environmental protection. In fact, I often remind my fellow Buddhists that the Buddha was not only born in the open air beneath a tree but also was enlightened in the shade of a tree and then
passed away under a tree. The image of nature, therefore, resonates
deeply in the paradigmatic story of Buddhist spirituality.

In relation to the inequities of poverty, the injunction to compassion
in all the world's major religions is an obvious and direct spur to action. Here Islam, with its emphasis on Zakat, or almsgiving, as one
of the Five Pillars, and Christianity with its remarkable tradition of
charity, are inspiring exemplars of how world religions can turn
their attention to the moral challenges of poverty and inequality.
In the monastic traditions—Christian, Buddhist, Jain, and Hindu—
there is shared emphasis on the simplicity of owning very little for
oneself. In the Buddhist form I know best, the precept states that the
only items I may really own for myself are those that are necessary
for my immediate use. If I meet someone more needy than me, as a
Buddhist monk I should give away even my own spare set of robes.
On the personal level, I have always found the huge inequity of
wealth that is so pervasive in our modern world to be deeply troubling. As adherents of a religious vision of life, or as people who take
compassion to be the defining quality of a human being, we need
constantly to confront this situation and to challenge our own com-
placencies about tolerating this gap. Not only is the gap increasing
on the global level between the north and the south, but within

individual nations, too, the phenomenon of economic inequity is on the rise. It is striking that, for example, Washington, D.C., the capital of the richest nation on earth, has pockets of poverty where people live in conditions of poor housing and ill-health that would hardly be tolerated in some of the poor countries of the Third World. Ironically, yawning gaps between the rich and the poor are opening up fast even in avowedly communist countries like China. This trend is increasing throughout the world, and unless we act soon there may come a point when it becomes irreversible. In terms of how we might counteract this tendency, clearly the leaders of the world religions must speak out consistently on the immorality of inequality. Here, I feel that Pope John Paul II, in the long years of his episcopacy, served as the conscience of the affluent north in repeatedly calling for aid to Africa, Asia, and South America. But on the level of the individual religious believer, each of us needs to take seriously a call for compassion issuing from our own faith traditions and do whatever we can practically to help our fellow brothers and sisters who are in greater need. All the religions have something to learn from Islam, which enshrines this charity as an obligation on the faithful, and from Sikhism, which insists so strongly on the value of service.

The question of scientific progress and the new ethical challenges it has thrown before us is particularly vexing for the faith traditions. Here, both the religions, as institutions, and their adherents, as individuals, face specific problems of adapting to unavoidable new realities without compromising fundamental ethical principles. Although the faithful must use their scriptures as a guide to the formulation of responses to new moral challenges, the religions cannot expect to find explicit or specific discussions of given technological innovations in these ancient scriptures. Yet the very antiquity of our religions demonstrates how, over time, they have successfully adapted to new challenges without undermining their fundamental nature. In rising to the demands of new realities, historically the faith traditions have relied on a combination of three factors: scripture as a model rooted in the essence of one's tradition, compassion as the value that underpins one's actions, and reason to navigate through the problems presented by new circumstances. The current challenge is not different in kind, but it is hugely complex because of the rapid pace of change and the enormity of power placed in human hands, which includes the possibilities of creating life in the laboratory, engineering new bio-organisms, and manipulating the very codes of life itself. Needless to say, all of these developments have far-reaching implications.

I see two ways in which the world's major religions can make a significant contribution. First, given their strong emphasis on ethics grounded in restraint and compassion, the world's faiths can serve as a reminder to the human species of the need for increased responsibility as we acquire greater knowledge and consequently greater power. This is vital because ethics function to balance responsibility against knowledge and power. The meaning of the word *responsibility* means the ability to respond appropriately to a given situation—which means with compassion, in the context of both religion-based and a nonreligious ethics. Second, in attempting to evolve an ethical model appropriate for these circumstances, our faith traditions collectively serve as humanity's richest and deepest spiritual resource. Because of the need for responsibility and the emphasis on compassion in each religion, we must set aside our doctrinal differences to find a common voice that offers an ethically grounded conceptual framework that can speak to the demands driving the new science. This way the world's religions can offer a means by which their ethical resources can be brought to bear upon the larger concerns of humanity. The nonreligious, too, whatever their attitudes toward religion, must embrace the collective ethical teachings of the world's faith traditions as essential to fundamental human values.

Religious and Secular: Can the Twain Meet?

Up until now, this book has concerned itself mainly with the relations between the world religions, the possibility for nonexclusivist inter-religious understanding between them, and collective action founded upon a shared ethics of compassion. But there is a further part of the picture, which is equally important when it comes to the welfare of humankind and the fate of the world we live in. Here, I mean the relationship between the religious and the nonreligious world. In essence, this is a question of the interface between two perspectives—one grounded in a worldview that includes the embrace of a supra-mundane dimension, the other rooted in an understanding of human existence as confined to our physical and biological reality.

When contrasting religious and secular here, I use the term *secular* in the way that active nonbelievers use it to refer to themselves. One of the great problems in the world—not only in relation to the various challenges of modernity but also in terms of world peace—is that these two parties, the religious and the secular, have for so long found it difficult, if not impossible, to talk to each other. Indeed, often each presents itself as by definition the opposite or reverse of the other.

The antipathy between the religious and the secular is exacerbated by mutual suspicion, hostility, and recrimination in that each blames the other for the woes of the world. For the secularist, the religions represent dogmatism, intransigence, and rejection of what is seen as the defining feature of the human mind—namely, critical reasoning. For the religious, secularism is what has led to excessive individualism, unbridled greed rooted in a materialist worldview, the breakdown of traditional family structures, and the loss of respect for anything that is sacred.

In a narrow sense, one could say that there is an element of truth in both these views. The contention that reason has no place in religion, however, is unfounded. To live fully according to the precepts of a religion's teachings involves a skillful balance of faith and reason, where one takes inspiration from the tradition but applies its teachings through the use of one's own critical judgment. Here, Pope Benedict XVI has rightly emphasized the need for the combination of faith and reason in one's religious life. In the language of Buddhism, this is the union of compassion and insight. At the same time, the charge that all the faults of modernity lie at the door of secularism is too simplistic, since greed and selfishness have been with us since time immemorial.

The problem with an atmosphere of mutual recrimination is not only that it serves to alienate people further but—much more important—the world faces crises for which this stance is actively unhelpful. On the personal level, whether we are secularist or religious, the challenges we face today touch us all. The bottom line is that peaceful coexistence, and the beneficial actions that can only arise from this, cannot be achieved without some measure of tolerance on all sides.

For the adherents of the world religions, once you embrace the spirit of pluralism, combined with the ethics of compassion, there is no reason to reject the common humanity of those who affirm a secular way of life. We may agree to differ on our professed beliefs (as different faiths differ between each other at the metaphysical level), but what matters is how we live our lives and the challenges we jointly face. On the part of the secularist, there is an obligation to respect the intelligence and sensibilities of millions of people for whom faith traditions speak deeply on what it means to be human. On both sides of the divide, there needs to be a softening of the hard edge of mutual rejection, with each narrowing intolerance of the other.

Instead of singling out the divisive history of the religions, nonbelievers must acknowledge the constructive and positive roles religion has played in the development of human culture, philosophy, and the transmission of knowledge. In the areas of social justice and freedom, too—from the abolition of slavery to the confrontation with communist totalitarianism in Europe during my lifetime—the significant contributions of the faith traditions cannot be ignored. Often, secularists identify religious conviction with a lack of scientific knowledge, and they assume that as rational understanding progresses, religious faith will gradually fade away. But this rests on a false premise. So long as human nature remains the way it is, with its needs and multiple afflictions of attachment, aversion, pride, and delusion that have been with us since memory began, the religions will continue to be relevant. In his great *Treasury of Higher Knowledge,* the fourth-century Indian sage Vasubandhu said that, of the constituents of the human mind, two are particular sources of conflict: *feelings* (or emotions), at the root of disputes on the everyday mundane level, and *discrimination* (or ideas), at the root of arguments at the intellectual level.

On a practical level, without inter-religious understanding, and without peace between secularists and adherents of religion, we cannot build a genuinely compassionate and happier humanity. So it is in the interests of those with a secular disposition not only to care for peaceful coexistence among the religions but also to actively work for tolerant acceptance of the religious world. Bluntly put, this is a matter of human happiness, world peace, and the survival of human beings as a species.

Let us be clear. The greatest challenge facing humankind today is the question of peaceful coexistence. As noted by Rabindranath Tagore in 1930, as I mentioned in the preface, no culture in the world can remain within its isolated citadel. From the globalized economic system to the intimately wired and instant nature of modern communications, from the mass movement of peoples and ideas to the collective challenges posed by the ecological crisis, from the creation of nuclear technology to the biochemical modifications of the very constituents of life itself, the forces pushing humanity into ever closer proximity are now much greater than Tagore could possibly have imagined. What will this pressure result in? It seems clear that either there will be an implosion with catastrophic consequences not just for the human species but also for the planet itself and all the other living beings with which we share the earth, or these forces will awaken us, even at this late hour, to a vision of a world where we relate to each other with a genuine openness of heart that embraces our differences within a spirit of the oneness of the human family.

For there to be true peaceful coexistence in the world, harmony among the world's major religions is indispensable. Seen in this light, the question of understanding among the faith traditions is no longer a matter that concerns religious believers alone. It affects the welfare of everyone on the planet. Nor is there space left for the secularists and the religious to enjoy the luxury of further bickering. I have always believed that the promotion of inter-religious under-standing is not only a response to the call for compassion from my own faith tradition but also a service to the well-being of humanity as a whole.

CONCLUSION

This book has traced the journey of a Buddhist monk who has had the precious opportunity to glimpse the vast expanse and multifaceted richness of the world's great religions. This journey has, without doubt, enriched my practice within my own Buddhist faith. In particular, the profound convergence of all the major religions on compassion has reinforced my conviction of the centrality of compassion as a universal spiritual value. In the face of the multiple paths, beliefs, and practices that the world's faith traditions offer, as a believer I have found myself confronting the question of my attitude toward the other faiths. I have come to feel that this is a question that all sincere adherents of religion must ask themselves, whatever their particular faith. Indeed, finding a balance between single-pointed commitment to one's own faith and genuine openness to the value of other faiths has come to be a deep personal quest. Over the course of the fifty years I have spent in India, a land where peaceful coexistence among religions has flourished for more than two thousand years, I have come to recognize that promotion of understanding among the world's religions is one of the most serious and important tasks facing the world today. In fact, alongside advocating fundamental human values, this task has come to occupy a great deal of my time, especially when I travel to different parts of the world.

In the course of this book, a central matter of concern has been the peaceful coexistence among peoples and their religions. None of us can any longer remain secure behind the walls and narrow confines of our specific culture and faith. Today the world we live in has become a very small place. In the face of this, we might throw up our arms at all the complications. Yet, as our world gets ever more complex and interconnected at all levels, the solution to its problems may be found somewhere very simple. Indeed, what could be more simple or more sustaining than to return to our basic human quality of empathy and good heart? On that level, all differences break down. Whether one is rich or poor, educated or illiterate, religious or nonbelieving, man or woman, black, white, or brown, we are all the same. Physically, emotionally, and mentally, we are all equal. We all share basic needs for food, shelter, safety, and love. We all aspire to happiness and we all shun suffering. Each of us has hopes, worries, fears, and dreams. Each of us wants the best for our family and loved ones. We all experience pain when we suffer loss and joy when we achieve what we seek. On this fundamental level, religion, ethnicity, culture, and language make no difference. Today's great challenge of peaceful coexistence demands that we remain in touch with this basic part of our nature.

One aspect of this approach involves situating any specific problems within a wider context. For example, when you are caught in a disagreement with someone, there is always the option to cause conflict. But there is also the option to see the contrasting views—one's own and the other's—in relation to the differing mental dispositions and aspirations that make up the wonderful diversity of the human family. In essence, what is required is the ability to recognize the truth in the interconnectedness of all things, even in our disagreements. The issue is not necessarily to see or go into all the intricate details of these connections; it is, rather, to acknowledge the big picture, to see any given event within that larger vision. So the process entails both returning to the basic simplicity of our shared human nature and looking out with the widest possible perspective. The shift of perspective alone can open the door of our hearts.

Let me conclude with an appeal. Of my fellow religious believers, I ask this. Obey the injunctions of your own faith; travel to the essence of your religious teaching, the fundamental goodness of the human heart. Here is the space where, despite doctrinal differences, we are all simply human. If you believe in God, see others as God's children. If you are a nontheist, see all beings as your mother. When you do this, there will be no room for prejudice, intolerance, or exclusivity. Make the vow today that you shall never allow your faith to be used as an instrument of violence. Make the vow today that you may become an instrument of peace, living according to the ethical teachings of compassion in your own religion. Open your heart so that the blessings of your faith may reach into its deepest recesses. To all people, religious and nonbelieving, I make this appeal. Always embrace the common humanity that lies at the heart of us all. Always affirm the oneness of our human family. Let your heart be softened by the balm of compassion, reflecting deeply upon the needs and aspirations of yourself and others. Let not your differences from the views of others come in the way of the wish for their peace, happiness, and well-being.

When we see another person, let us feel our basic affinity. In this place, there are no strangers—all are brothers and sisters in their journeys through life. We are but temporary guests on this earth. At most, our lives span a hundred years. Within the great age of our shared planet, this is but a hiccup or a breath of breeze. If we remain bogged down in divisions and perpetuate discord, how trivial a way this is to spend the brief time allotted us. Time never stops. So let us use it wisely in the service of others, or at least without contributing to their woes. Then, as the last day approaches, we can look back and rejoice, "Ah, I have made my existence meaningful." At the least we will have no regrets.

Our need to find a way of transcending our differences in order to live in peaceful coexistence is most urgent. For if we fail, and if our differences continue to lead to discord, and discord to violence, the consequences may be catastrophic. The stakes are higher than ever—not only for the survival of our species but also for the very planet itself and the myriad other creatures who share our home. The great power and knowledge we have places us in a position of unique responsibility. Today, even on the individual level, what we think about others who are different and how we live our lives have implications far beyond our immediate surroundings, with ramifications in a global dimension. This is the reality of the world we live in.

The only appropriate, responsible, and effective way to live in this undeniable reality is to follow the principles of compassion. At a minimum, each of us must live our life upholding the regard for others at our core. Let me end with the beautiful words of Shantideva:

May the fearful become fearless;
May those oppressed by grief find joy;
May those who are anxious
Be rid of their anxiety and feel secure.

May health come to the sick;
May they be free from every bondage;
May those who are weak find strength,
Their minds tender towards each other.

As long as space remains,
As long as sentient beings remain,
Until then, may I too remain
And help dispel the miseries of the world.
(BODHICARYAVATARA, CHAPTER X)

May peace and happiness prevail everywhere!

In this book, we have made the following choices in citing scriptures written in languages other than English:

PRIMARY SCRIPTURES

Buddhism

Dharmasutra of Gautama. *Dharmasutras: The Law Codes of Ancient India.* A new translation by Patrick Olivelle (Oxford World Classics, Oxford University Press, 1999).

Dhammapada. Translation by Valerie J. Roebuck (London: Penguin, scheduled August 2010).

Metta Sutta, from the Sutta Nipata. Translation by Thanissaro Bhikkhu, available at www.accesstoinsight.org.

Theravada Buddhism, Pali canon. See www.accesstoinsight.org. For texts and translations of early Buddhist scriptures in languages

other than Pali (including Udana), see www.ancient-buddhist-etexts
.net/texts-and-translations/TT-index.htm.

Udanavarga, Gandavyuha Sutra, and other classical Indian and Tibetan
Buddhist sources cited here. Translation by Thupten Jinpa, principal English translator to the Dalai Lama.

Hinduism

Upanishads. Translation by Valerie J. Roebuck (London: Penguin,
2003).

Ramayana of Valimik, including Yuddha Kanda. Translation by Hari
Prasad Shastri (London: Shanti Sadan, 1952–9).

Bhagavad Gita. Translation by W. J. Johnson (London: Oxford University Press, 2009).

Dharmasutra

Mahabharata

Shiva Mahapurana, including Rudra Samhita. Translated by Shanti Lal
Nagar (Delhi: Parimal, 2007).

Jainism

Tattvarthasutra. *That Which Is: Tattvartha Sutra.* The Sacred Literature
Series, translated by Nathmal Tatia (Harper Collins, 1994).

Sutrakritanga

Sikhism

Adi Granth. *The Holy Adhi Granth,* a comparison of several translations
of this sacred text into English is available online at www.sikhs.org/
english/frame.html.

Judaism

Talmud. The Babylonian Talmud in translation, available at www.come
-and-hear.com/navigate.html.

Zohar. Pritzker Edition, translated by Daniel C. Matt (Palo Alto: Stanford University Press, 2004).

Christianity

Holy Bible. The New International Version, available online in a searchable form alongside many other versions in numerous languages at www.biblegateway.com.

Islam

Holy Qur'an. Translation by N. J. Dawood, revised edition (London: Penguin, 1999).

Hadith. Translated versions available at www.iiu.edu.my/deed/hadith and www.edu./schools/college/cree/engagement/resources/texts/muslim/hadith.

Daoism

Daodejing by Laozi. Translation by Benjamin Penny and Edmund Ryden (London: Oxford University Press, 2008).

Tai-shang Kan-ying Píen

Confucianism

The Analects. Version in *A Source Book in Chinese Philosophy*, translated and compiled by Wing-tsit Chan (Princeton, N.J.: Princeton University Press, 1963).

Zoroastrianism

Dadisten-I-dinik

OTHER TEXTS CITED

Ashoka's inscriptions. *Ashoka and the Decline of the Mauryas*, translated by Romila Tharpar (New Delhi: Oxford University Press, 1997), Appendix V.

Songs of Kabir. Translated by Rabindranath Tagore and Introduction by Evelyn Underhill (New York: The Macmillan Company, 1915).

Martin Kitchen, *Word of Promise* (Canterbury Press, 1998).

Judah Loew

Thomas Merton, *Asian Journal*

Milarepa's poem. *Songs of Spiritual Experience: Tibetan Buddhist Poems of Insight and Awakening,* by Thupten Jinpa and Jaś Elsner (Boston: Shambhala, 2000).

Mirabai's songs. *Mirabai: Ecstatic Poems,* translated by Robert Bly and Jane Hirschfield (Boston: Beacon Press, 2004).

Nagarjuna's *Precious Garland.* Translated by Thupten Jinpa.

Palu Ju's poems. Translated by Thupten Jinpa.

Pirke Avot. Translation available at www.shechem.org/torah/avot.html.

Rumi's songs. *Rumi's World: The Life and Works of the Greatest Sufi Poet,* translated by Annemarie Schimmel, with slight adaptation (Boston: Shambhala, 1992).

Prayer of St. Francis of Assissi. Version available at www.catholic-forum .com

Shantideva's *Bodhicaryavatara.* Translation by Paul Williams, Kate Crosby, and Andrew Skilton (London: Oxford University Press, 1995), with modifications by Thupten Jinpa.

Saint John of the Cross. *The Collected Works of St. John of the Cross,* translated by Kieran Kavanaugh and Otilio Rodriquez (Washington, D.C.: ICS, 1991).

Rabindranath Tagore, *The Religion of Man* (New York: The Macmillan Company, 1931).

The Asian Journal of Thomas Merton (New York: New Directions Press, 1973).

ACKNOWLEDGMENTS

The editors would like to express their sincere thanks to the following individuals who have read either parts or the entirety of the manuscript and offered helpful critical comments: Robert Chodos, Ngari Rinpoché Tenzin Choegyal, Geshe Dorje Damdul, Father Richard Finn, Silvia Frenk, K. C. Branscomb Kelley, Bilal Kushner, Sophie Boyer Langri, Geshe Lhakdor Lobsang Jordan, Rajiv Mehrotra, Sarah Shaw, and, last but not least, Tenzin Geyche Tethong, who served as the private secretary to His Holiness the Dalai Lama for over four decades.

Thupten Jinpa and Jaś Elsner, editors